THE
MESSAGE
BEHIND THE
MOVIE

THE
MESSAGE
BEHIND THE
MOVIE

HOW TO ENGAGE WITH A FILM
WITHOUT DISENGAGING YOUR FAITH

DOUGLAS M.
BEAUMONT

MOODY PUBLISHERS

Chicago

© 2009 by
Douglas M. Beaumont

Editor: Christopher Reese
Interior Design: Smartt Guys design
Cover Design: The Designworks Group, Inc.
Cover Image: Veer #PDP0939047
Author Photo: D Kenney Imaging

Library of Congress Cataloging-in-Publication Data
Beaumont, Douglas M.
 The message behind the movie : how to engage with a film without
disengaging your faith / Douglas M. Beaumont.
  p. cm.
 Includes bibliographical references.
 ISBN 978-0-8024-3201-8
 1. Motion pictures--Moral and ethical aspects. 2. Motion
pictures--Religious aspects--Christianity. I. Title.
 PN1995.5.B36 2009
 261.5'7--dc22

                    2009003919

We hope you enjoy this book from Moody Publishers. Our goal is to provide high-quality, thought-provoking books and products that connect truth to your real needs and challenges. For more information on other books and products written and produced from a biblical perspective, go to www.moodypublishers.com or write to:

Moody Publishers
820 N. LaSalle Boulevard
Chicago, IL 60610

1 3 5 7 9 10 8 6 4 2

Printed in the United States of America

This book is dedicated to my wife, Elaine.
Thank you for your trust in God,
your belief in me,
your commitment to us,
your example of excellence,
your sacrificial love,
your hard work,
and for our wonderful son, Michael.

CONTENTS

Movies Are **Important**

Movies matter because they are the primary art, storytelling, and entertainment medium of our time.

Art is the means through which human beings respond to the cosmos. The impulse to make something beautiful that will last, and that will make sense of life and experience, is uniquely human. It is the task of every generation to bequeath something to future generations to inspire them, to encourage them, and perhaps to caution them. In art, people reach across the boundaries of culture and time to create, what the poet and playwright Pope John Paul II called "new epiphanies of beauty," as a loving legacy for people yet to be born.

Stories are the preferred way human beings learn and define our values. In our stories we find heroes whose larger than life examples make heroism possible in our own small struggles. A society without stories has no dreams, no nobility, no challenge, no depth.

Entertainment is the way we stretch ourselves beyond the limits of our work-a-day lives to experience the full potential of our human nature. Our entertainment should lead us to laugh hard, to cry with empathy, to shudder in fear at evil, and to feel delight and wonder.

A great movie is at once a harmonious and radiant work of art, a story with a profound and universal truth, and an exhilarating emotional journey. The potential of the movie screen to be all these things makes it a gift to our modern age, and a vital element in the church's task of cultural and social evangelism.

Hollywood matters as the global center of moviemaking. It makes no sense that Christians would be missing from this unbelievably influential and urgent landscape, or that we would ignore and avoid its products. Believers have something to say that is sorely absent in Hollywood at the dawn of the twenty-first century. Namely, we could bring a note of hope to the art, stories, and entertainment that is going out on the screens of the world. We could counteract the cynicism that pervades so many movies in which it seems that good and evil are somehow equal in power, or even that darkness is stronger than the light. We could create stories that expose the relentless rationalizations and despair of the pervasive culture of death. We could assert with beauty and potency that suffering isn't the worst thing that can happen to a human being, and that the loss of integrity or the loss of the soul is much, much worse. All of this our culture sorely needs to hear from us through the art and storytelling medium of our time.

But if we have learned anything in the cinema-making efforts of Christians in recent years, it is that you can't make beautiful movies unless you understand and love the medium. You can't love and understand something you fear, or disdain, or dismiss.

Christians seem to fall into two camps regarding Hollywood and our whole media-saturated contemporary culture. There are those I think of as the Cave-Dwelling Christians, and those who swagger around as the Teflon Christians. Both are oversimplifications of the complex feat of gleaning and negotiation required to be an effective disciple surrounded by the media in today's world.

The Cave-Dwelling Christians proudly declare that they never watch television or go to the movies. "It's all garbage!" they proclaim with a thin veneer of superiority. They are wrong. There are many wonderful movies being made today, which could be a source of comfort and inspiration to these folks, if only they were watching. The Cave Dwellers are afraid of being scandalized and violated by something on the screen, so they shut out everything on the screen. It's a kind of laziness in which they can't be bothered to seek out the wheat from amidst the tares, so they root up the whole crop. There is also a touch of resentment and elitism that taints many religious people who reject everything the mostly unbelieving artists and storytellers of the modern world might have to say. Finally, there is a profound ignorance in many religious people of how to critically appraise a movie. It's so much easier to dismiss the movies as being a waste than to admit that "pagan Hollywood" has perfected a very complex and powerful set of storytelling and aesthetic skills that are way, way beyond you. It all smacks so much of Aesop's The Fox and the Grapes: "Who needs the movies? They would probably make me sick."

The Teflon Christians, on the other hand, consume everything the modern culture has to serve with a hubristic shrug. These folks go around saying with a dismissive roll of the eyeballs, "It's just a movie. Get over it." They either think they are immune from being violated by the screen, or they have just grown too lazy to try to sort out the good from the bad. In the worst cases, they imbibe all the sewage the culture has to offer with a salacious fan-enjoyment that is no different from the ancient Romans hooting over the gladiators. At best, they are living their lives with their fingers crossed, hoping that a lifetime of *Desperate Housewives*, *World Wrestling SmackDown*, and *Grand Theft Auto* will somehow leave them and their children still pure and holy on the day the Lord returns.

Both of these profiles are wrong ways for disciples to live. The truth is, while movies are easy to watch, their impact and messages are often much more difficult to apprehend. It is a shame when a Christian gives an unqualified approval to the positive messages in *The 40-Year-Old Virgin* or *Little Miss Sunshine*, but doesn't even stop to wonder if the crassness in the storytelling method in both those films undermines them. It's a bigger shame when Christians pan a movie like *In the Bedroom* because it is about a revenge murder, and miss the profound theme in the piece about the need to forgive. I am continually astounded by how few people can read a theme in a movie, or how many completely miss the way a skilled filmmaker controls and manipulates the viewer's sympathies by orchestrating the camera's point of view. In a cultural moment defined by screen media, it is remarkable how ignorant most people—particularly people of faith—are about how screen stories work. We believers are supposed to have our eyes trained on "the signs of the times" as open doors for evangelism. The movies are the "signs" of our times. We aren't supposed to be shutting out the world, or losing ourselves in it. It is bad for the world that Christians are bad at making and reading movies. It is bad for Christians that they are missing the depth and beauty of the art and stories that are being made all around them.

This current volume goes a long way in helping today's moviegoer navigate the wonderful and complex medium of the motion picture. Douglas Beaumont clearly loves the cinematic art form, and sets his admiring glance on the filmmakers' techniques as much as their messages. This is very refreshing in the annals of Christian film commentaries, which tend to muse only on story points. This book is an ample and enjoyable primer for Christians wanting to engage the movies in a spirit of appreciation but also critical appraisal. It will help Christians move beyond fear and ignorance of Hollywood into a posture of respect and, hopefully, even grudging gratitude. It will increase your enjoyment of this art form, and help you get so much more out of the stories being told on the screen. And finally, this book will hopefully lead many people of faith to pray and work for a new renaissance in Hollywood and the movies.

The movies aren't going away. We need to master them as consumers and producers so that, far from considering Hollywood an enemy, future generations of believers will see the screen as just a bigger and better delivery system for a new set of parables for a world hungering for meaning and beauty.

BARBARA R. NICOLOSI
Founding director of Act One, a training program for Hollywood writers and executives, and adjunct professor of screenwriting at Azusa Pacific University

"The author of a work of imagination is trying to affect us wholly, as human beings, whether he knows it or not; and we are affected by it, as human beings, whether we intend to be or not."

– T. S. Eliot

What's the Story?

One of the most difficult courses for me in seminary was homiletics (or "preaching"). I guess I just didn't have the gift. But one thing I did get out of the class was an appreciation for stories, and especially how a good story can affect its hearers. Much of what makes a story good is, of course, how it is told. I needed some work on this, so my professor suggested I look into screenwriting. So I read a few books. Then a few more. Then several more. Then everything I could get my hands on. I thought this was information that others could use to better understand and enjoy the movies they were watching. Fortunately Steve Lyon and Paul Santhouse at Moody Publishers thought so, too. Their patience and shared vision concerning this book are much appreciated.

I am now a seminary teacher, a Christian apologist, an armchair philosopher, and a backseat theologian. While I am not a director, screenwriter, or gaffer, I am a big movie fan. Though I would not call myself a cinephile (the official term for "movie geek"), I have spent a fair amount of time in front of the silver screen. Therefore I write as an evangelical, philosophical, theological, movie lover. *The Message Behind the Movie* is my attempt to unite my interest in theology, philosophy, and apologetics with my love of film. Perhaps it will be the catalyst for you that my homiletics class was for me.

During my research for this book, I discovered that professional screenwriters often follow a standard system when writing film screenplays. Act One (chapters 1-6) explains how this system works and will equip you to be a more actively engaged moviegoer. Meanwhile, I also discovered that engaging movies actively can provide a Christian with an extraordinary opportunity for doing evangelism (proclaiming the faith) and apologetics (defending the faith). So in Act Two (chapters 7-10), I discuss several common objections and challenges to the Christian faith and demonstrate how films can be an excellent means of launching conversations in which these issues can be addressed. Act Three (chapter 11) wraps it all up with biblical advice on choosing which movies to watch and which ones to avoid.

It is said that stealing from one author is plagiarism but stealing from several authors is research. There is some truth to this; I have certainly benefited from standing on the shoulders of some of the giants in the film industry and Christian ministry. In addition to the materials I read in preparation for this writing (see Resources), my thinking on the primary subjects of this book has been most influenced by Brian Godawa in his helpful conversations about the film business, and the faculty of Southern Evangelical Seminary who taught me the foundations and defense of the faith.

Special thanks goes out to my dad for introducing me to Monty Python and explaining Chekhov's Gun (although we didn't know it was called that); to my mom for letting me stay up and watch scary movies when I was probably too young for that sort of thing; to my movie-watching crews throughout the years; and to Nathan Pierce for his valuable research and suggestions. Finally, my ongoing gratitude goes out to the creators of my favorite films and to my wife, Elaine, whom I got to know during many of them.

ACT ONE

WATCHING
& UNDERSTANDING
MOVIES

Can Anything **Good**
Come Out of Hollywood?

Coffee Shop Talk:

A NON-DATE AT CAFÉ VERITAS

Mike Schonberg and Nita Wellborn were definitely *not* on a date, as they found chairs next to a window overlooking the parking lot of Café Veritas. Outside, everything was taking on a reddish glow as the sun dropped below the skyline, silhouetting the ornate tower of the old movie theater across the street. This was their first "get-together," and although both insisted that it was not a date, their friends in the college group teased them mercilessly (as good friends seem obligated to do). Mike was glad they had settled on an after school visit to the café–it was cozy and private at this time of day. As they settled into their overstuffed chairs, Mike racked his brain for something to talk about. Why did his mind always seem to shift into neutral in the presence of an attractive girl? He gazed across the parking lot and spied the movie theater. Perfect!

"Seen any good movies lately?" he asked, at once proud of himself for preventing an awkward silence and embarrassed for having to resort to a cliché.

"I don't really like movies," Nita answered casually. When she saw Mike's look of surprise, she felt the need to explain. "I just think movies are a waste of time. All that sex and violence, and for what? They never have anything good to say. In fact, most of them—even the ones for kids—seem to promote evil. It just seems like Christians should have better things to do with their time." She immediately wished she hadn't added that last part. What if Mike was a movie nut? Their first date (make that "get-together"), and she'd probably just insulted him!

Mike was not surprised by this answer; he'd heard it before and had a ready response. "Well, everyone takes time out for entertainment. I know there is a lot of bad stuff in movies, but I'm able to filter it out pretty well. If a movie is really bad, I can always get up and leave."

"Have you ever actually done that?" Nita asked, wondering why she was starting to feel defensive.

Mike thought about it. "Well, no—not really." He noticed a slightly triumphant gleam in Nita's eye.

She continued her interrogation. "So, you're telling me you have never watched a movie so awful that you had to leave? What's the worst movie you ever sat through?"

Now Mike was in a bind. He knew he had seen some pretty bad stuff. So he decided to dodge. "Well, most of the time I'm with friends and don't want to embarrass them." That sounded pretty good. But Nita was one step ahead of him.

"What kind of friends do you hang around with who would be embarrassed by your walking out of a movie?"

Mike was mentally sweating now, but Nita's question gave him an idea—a change of tactic. "I find that movies are a way to find common ground with my non-believing friends. Don't you think we need to be able to interact with the culture?" There! He had turned the conversation around.

Nita only looked confused. "What do you mean? Should Christians involve themselves in sin just so they can be buddies with non-believers? How is that showing Christ to the world?"

This was going poorly. *What was the big deal?* Mike thought. *Didn't everyone like at least a few movies?* Surely. "Are there any movies you *have* liked, Nita?" He hoped this would get them on the same side.

Nita looked suspicious, but thought for a minute and managed to come up with something. "This is probably going to sound stupid to you, but I did like . . ." she trailed off.

Mike jumped at the opportunity to get this conversation back on friendly ground. "No, please tell me!"

Nita eyed him for a moment, and then said, "*The Wizard of Oz.* I liked it when I was a kid, and I guess I still do." She looked back and grinned sheepishly. "Happy?"

Mike smiled. Although he would never admit it in front of his friends, he had loved that movie when he was a kid, too. He breathed a sigh of relief and was about to remark on the coincidence when a thought occurred to him. Against his better judgment he offered Nita a small challenge: "Um, but doesn't *The Wizard of Oz* have violence and witchcraft in it?" He grinned as he said it, hoping she would not take his question too seriously. It sort of worked.

"Oh, come on," Nita responded, laughing, "you can't compare *The Wizard of Oz* to the junk in movie theaters today. It's a classic kid's story!"

Mike saw an opportunity to have some fun and hopefully regain some of his lost moral ground. "A minute ago you said that you didn't like movies because of violence and sinful messages. So how come you have no problem justifying those things in a movie that *you* like?"

Nita opened her mouth to speak, and then abruptly shut it.

Ha! Mike thought, *I've got her!* He was just leaning back to take his first sip of coffee when Nita answered, "*The Wizard of Oz* doesn't have cussing or nudity, and it certainly does not promote evil. That's what makes it different."

Mike knew that she was right at some level, but he was not about to let her off that easy. "Well, *The Wizard of Oz* is violent though, right? The scarecrow catches fire, the dog tries to bite that lady, the witch melts—which freaked me out when I was a kid! Not to mention the witch herself. She was scary!"

Nita paused, bit her lip, and then answered, "Well, the violence was pretty tame compared to movies today . . . and the witch was *supposed* to be scary, because she was evil!"

"So if a movie has some violence and witchcraft, it's OK as long as the witch is clearly evil?"

"Yes," Nita replied.

"I guess you're right," Mike said as he reflected for a moment, then added, "but wasn't there also a *good* witch?"

Nita's mouth opened and remained open as her eyes focused past him for a moment. She had thought her last response was going to be the end of this conversation. Now what? How could she defend her favorite movie's portrayal of witchcraft as a good thing?

Deep down Mike thought Nita was probably right. And Nita believed she was missing something, but she just couldn't find the right words to express it. Mike was looking at her with a smirk growing on his lips. She shot him with her straw wrapper, and they changed the subject.

HOORAY FOR HOLLYWOOD?

Do you sympathize more with Mike or Nita? Both had good reasons for their perspectives on the subject of movies, but who was right? The fact that you are reading this book suggests that you perceive some value in movies. But perhaps, like many Christians, you are uncertain how to think about movies as they relate to your Christian beliefs.

Like Nita, some Christians choose to simply dismiss nearly everything that comes out of Hollywood as pure evil.[1] These abstainers usually watch very few movies and are extremely critical when they do, often focusing on the style elements of movies more than anything else. While this position is not difficult to sympathize with, given the content of many movies these days, it does have negative consequences. Movies often provide us with new words, phrases, or references that can be very helpful for connecting with others. By avoiding movies altogether, Nita and others may be unaware of shifts in current popular-level thinking, thereby limiting their ability to connect with the people they go to school or work with.

On the other end of the spectrum are those who have an almost careless affinity for movies. These folks are more concerned with entertainment than style. "It's just good fun," they will say. "Don't take things so seriously!" These people will watch practically anything, tolerate practically anything, and view most films uncritically. They will often ignore offensive style elements so long as they are entertained. Perhaps worse, they may not think they are being affected by the films they watch. Because they don't think critically about movies, these viewers are often unable to say anything more about a movie than whether or not they enjoyed it. Unlike the movie abstainers, movie lovers may be able to make more inside cultural references, but they often cannot connect movies to deeper issues.

In the dialogue above, Mike represents yet another approach to movies. People like Mike recognize the cultural importance of movies and may be inclined to celebrate anything with a spiritual theme, whether real or imagined. In their desire to see movies used for spiritual purposes, movie advocates sometimes ignore the clear message of a movie and impose a spiritual message upon it. Advocates may even be glad to see that there were no overt Christian elements in a movie as long as there were, at some allegorical level, spiritual themes. The danger of this approach is that movie advocates sometimes fail to see the actual message of a movie in their quest for spiritual relevance and, consequently, may champion a film with a message that is antithetical to their beliefs.

As this brief survey shows, there is little consensus among Christians concerning how to think about movies.

THE CHURCH'S PLATONIC RELATIONSHIP WITH MOVIES

It may encourage you to know that this debate is nothing new. Disagreement over movies is in many ways a contemporary version of a debate about the influence of art that has raged since long before the first moving picture was ever conceived.

Historically, there have been two competing positions regarding the purpose of art and the proper way to judge its worth, positions which originate with philosophers Plato and Aristotle. Both men admitted to delighting in art, but they had very different ideas about art's ultimate effects. Most important for us, their differences help explain why Christians can disagree about the value of film.[2]

To put it simply, Plato viewed art as largely useless and, oftentimes, even harmful. This assessment was based on the philosopher's understanding of virtue and goodness. Plato believed that to be virtuous, a person must have true knowledge. If art only imitates truth—but is not actually true—it cannot make a person truly virtuous. He also believed that the highest good is also the most *real*. Because all art is essentially an imitation of reality (and often a faulty imitation), it is not morally neutral, but is actually bad.[3] Finally, art can be dangerous, because its "language" (whether music, poetry, painting, or something else) is emotionally provocative. When the passions are aroused, the soul's balance is disrupted and a person becomes irrational. For these reasons, said Plato, people should only be exposed to art that strongly and clearly communicates ultimate truths.

Plato's student Aristotle thought of art differently. While he agreed that art imitates reality, he did not consider this a problem. Artistic imitation is one way humans distinguish themselves from the lower animals, and that makes it a good thing for humans to do. Art is also useful for learning, even when it depicts immoral behavior. For example, a comedy depicting fools and their folly is useful because it can teach us to avoid foolishness (which is good) without our having to make foolish decisions (which is bad). Aristotle also noted that art has cathartic value; that is, it can help us release the very emotions that it arouses, so that we ultimately achieve the balance Plato thought was lost when the passions are inflamed. For example, viewing violence may make us more compassionate toward the victims of violence.

Finally, Aristotle recognized that art can actually describe ultimate reality more effectively precisely because it is not bound by mundane reality. As we all know, examples of virtue are sometimes hard to find in the real world. The virtue of courage, for instance, can often be more easily taught by watching a movie like *The Lord of the Rings* than by watching politicians on CNN. In other words, art can communicate profound truths about reality.

When it comes to movies, it appears that many Christians have agreed with Plato. We want films that communicate truth clearly without displaying anything bad. We want movies that have a strong, easily discernable moral message that does not arouse our "lower" passions. So when a film comes along that presents the dark side of life, asks more questions than it answers, portrays sinfulness, or excites our emotions, Christians may judge it as immoral. As I will argue, that's not always the correct response—we often must look deeper to discern the underlying message of a film. Think, for example, if movies were made of every book in the Bible. Some of these films would include portrayals of sinful behaviors and attitudes. How might film versions of Ecclesiastes, Job, Judges, Psalms, Song of Songs, or Revelation be produced?

Instead of following Plato exclusively, I think Christians would do well to recognize the merits of Aristotle's perspective. An Aristotelian approach to movies needn't condone sinfulness; instead, it can recognize how central storytelling is to human experience and seek to accurately critique the messages that stories in films are communicating.

DEEP IMPACT

Today more than ever before, popular culture may have a bigger impact on people than their family or church. Consider this: one study reported that teenagers spend about ten hours per day consuming media of various kinds. This means that even if teens were to spend two hours per day with their parents, by the end of the week they would have spent five times as much time immersed in media.[4] By the time a person in America reaches the age of eighteen, they've spent about forty thousand hours consuming media versus about eight thousand with parents and four thousand hours at church, if they attended regularly.

As early as the 1930s, one theater critic wrote, "Theaters are the new Church of the Masses—where people sit huddled in the dark listening to people in the light tell them what it is to be human."[5] In other words, movies encourage community by creating shared experiences that unite people as they try to make sense of the world—which means movies serve a function similar to that of religion. That is to say, for better or worse, movies can shape the way we think about the world. This can be a good thing. For example, and to echo Aristotle's observations about art in general, movies serve as a vicarious means of experiencing life. We can encounter things through movies that we might not otherwise get a chance to explore. This goes beyond mere entertainment. Movies provide a way to experience a myriad of situations with a measure of detachment that is impossible in real life. Rather than being shocked and ill-equipped to deal with these situations when they arise, it can be beneficial to safely explore these issues through cinema before being faced with them in real life.

CINEVANGELISM?

Because movies explore issues central to human experience, they can provide an excellent means of engaging people in conversation about the Christian faith. Much of my experience and training is in apologetics, the art of defending and explaining the Christian faith to non-Christians. So one of the primary ways I have found to integrate film into my life and ministry is to understand movies as communicators of current thought that can aid my understanding and conversing with contemporary culture.

Any relationship requires common ground, whether that is speaking the same language, living in the same neighborhood, or sharing a work environment or common interests. Sometimes this common ground has to be cultivated. Certainly we must avoid associating with non-Christians in an ungodly way that blurs our distinctions (2 Corinthians 6:14) and ruins our witness. But the best evangelists know that finding common ground means meeting people right where they are. In Acts 2, for example, Peter spoke to the crowds in Jerusalem using Old Testament prophecies to prove that Christ was the Messiah. But in Acts 17, when Paul was at Mars Hill, he used Greek philosophical arguments from creation to lead the pagan philosophers to Christ. In both cases, the success of the evangelism was directly related to the speaker's ability to make use of cultural connections through the power of the Holy Spirit.

More often than not, these cultural connections can be found in a culture's stories. Ursula K. LeGuin writes that "story . . . is one of the basic tools invented by the mind of man, for the purpose of gaining understanding. There have been great societies that did not use the wheel, but there are no societies that did not tell stories."[6] In the same way that we can investigate ancient cultures through their stories, we can learn much about our own through films. Movies make us conversant with the great stories of our time. Like tales spun around the campfires of our forefathers, movies draw us together and give us a common story. At a time when religion is distrusted as a source for ultimate truth, movies allow us to collectively reflect on our own stories and share our reflections with other viewers.

In order to successfully integrate movies into our spiritual lives, though, we first need to learn how to evaluate movies, so that we neither miss the good nor uncritically accept the bad. It may sound like a tough job, but with some basic guidelines, anyone can make objective judgments of a movie's worth. When this process becomes natural, you will begin to see things you might never have noticed or appreciated in films before. You might find that this training helps you enjoy movies more, in the same way that musicians often have a greater appreciation for music than do those of us who don't play an instrument. Even so, increasing our pleasure in movie watching is not our primary goal. Rather, we are concerned primarily with learning to evaluate a movie in light of our Christian beliefs. So we will learn to discern a movie's message or significance as revealed by its story, including how that story is told (its style) and what worldview it assumes (its suppositions). Whether a movie presents a strong Christian, non-Christian, or anti-Christian world-view, we need to be prepared to address its worldview in our conversations. Therefore, the second part of this book will feature basic lessons in message evaluation and response.

SHOULD CHRISTIANS BE INVOLVED IN SECULAR ENTERTAINMENT AT ALL?

Even if we acknowledge the possible positive influence of movies, we may still wonder whether we should consume products created by non-Christian culture. If we follow the example of the apostle Paul, the answer appears to be "yes." Consider the following Scripture verses:

- *"Meats for the belly, and the belly for meats."*
- *"Let us eat and drink, for tomorrow we die."*
- *"Bad company corrupts good character."*
- *"Cretans are always liars."*
- *"It hurts you to kick against the goads."*
- *"In him we live and move and have our being . . . for we too are his offspring."*

In order, these quotations are from 1 Corinthians 6:13 (KJV); 15:32 (KJV); 15:33 (NIV); Titus 1:12 (NIV); and Acts 26:14 (NRSV); 17:28 (NRSV). What may surprise you is that in each of these verses, the Holy Spirit inspired Paul to quote pagan writers![7] In fact, in its original form, the last quote refers to Zeus![8] Yet God saw fit to use the statement to communicate the truth of the gospel when Paul spoke to the Greeks, whose authors penned those words. It seems, then, that Christians can utilize truth communicated in non-Christian culture to further God's kingdom.

WHY DO YOU CALL IT "GOOD"?

"Is that a good movie?" can be a dangerous question. We use the word "good" to refer to pizza, dogs, books, and God. Clearly, we don't always use this word in the same way. If two people do not agree on what makes something "good," they will surely reach different conclusions. This is especially true for movies. There are any number of elements that people judge movies by (artistic styling, acting quality, storytelling, special effects, musical score, a moral message, etc.). In addition, nothing on this earth is perfect, so anything we evaluate will be a mixture of good and bad. For this reason, movies that some consider "good" should not necessarily be viewed by all people. *The Exorcist* (1973), for example, ultimately portrays the triumph of faith, which is a good message. Yet the film's depictions of evil are so horrific that they might not be worth enduring for the sake of the film's good message. There is often a fine line between the good a film contains and the objectionable elements one must endure to get to it. This topic is covered in more detail in chapters 4 and 11.

In light of these considerations, we need to keep in mind that saying a movie is "good" can mean that a film is well-done, or that it affirms a biblical worldview, or simply that a viewer enjoyed it. Throughout the book, I will sometimes make positive comments about movies for the skill with which they use various elements to tell a story and convey their overarching message. Please understand that I am not attempting to provide a guide for which specific movies are acceptable for you to watch. Rather, I will present principles that can help you make informed and Christ-honoring movie-watching decisions.

In either case, my purpose in this book is to show how we can all better interact with our culture by understanding the movies that shape and reveal it. In order to do this well, I will cite a wide variety of movies as illustrations of various points. However, unless I specifically state my overall evaluation of these movies, my use of them as examples should not be understood as either a general recommendation or condemnation.

CONCLUSION

I hope that this book will help you avoid careless affinity, unnecessary abstinence, and overzealous advocacy of films by focusing on how movies communicate their message. This will allow us to evaluate films more objectively. Then we can appreciate and utilize movies for what they are, even when they are not what we might like them to be. Author Stephen Lawhead once wrote, "Those who reject popular culture wholly or in part tend to see the devil as extremely active in the world, so terrible in his power and influence that the best defense is retreat."[9] His advice, and mine, on the subject is neatly summarized in the quote below.

MONSIGNOR: | *"Now we must all fear evil men. But there is another kind of evil that we must fear most. And that is the indifference of good men."* (The Boondock Saints)

REFLECTION QUESTIONS

1. *What are the benefits and pitfalls of approaching movies like Plato or Aristotle would?*

2. *How did the apostle Paul adapt his evangelism style when he spoke with Jewish people or Gentiles (e.g., Acts 17)?*

3. *When might it be best to avoid watching a "good" movie?*

How a Story Is Told
vs. What a Story Tells

HOW TO WATCH A MOVIE

In 1972 philosopher Mortimer Adler published a book titled *How to Read a Book*. Adler knew, of course, that at some level every literate person can read a book. But he also knew that some people read better than others. Some readers skim paragraphs, skip sections, or pay little attention to how a paragraph relates to the ones before and after it. Other readers engage the book before them more actively. They read not just to pass the time, but to learn something. To do this they pay careful attention to the structure, form, and content of the book they are reading. In the end, the better a person reads, the more likely they are to enjoy reading.

What is true of reading books is also true of watching movies. In a sense, anyone can watch a movie, if by "watch" they simply mean sitting in front of a flashing screen. But there is more to the experience of watching a movie than passively receiving images. Fortunately, with a little instruction, anyone can learn to watch movies well.

Now, the idea of "learning to watch movies" might sound intimidating or even boring. But just as learning to read more carefully makes books more enjoyable, knowing more about movies actually makes them more entertaining. Not only that, knowledgeable moviegoers can become better acquainted with their culture than those who only enter the theater to be entertained.

One of the first steps in the process of becoming a thoughtful moviegoer is learning to discern the difference between how someone tells a story and what that person is telling us with the story. To cite a biblical example, think for a moment about Jesus' account of the prodigal son in Luke 15:11-32. Essentially, the message of the parable—what Jesus is telling us with the story—is that God loves His children deeply and unconditionally. But Jesus' method of communicating that message—how He tells the story—is to create characters with relationships and place them in a first-century setting where they behave in certain ways. If we assume that Jesus' method of telling the story means that it is simply a tale of a man and his two sons, we miss His point completely.

We'll explore the specific methods moviemakers use to tell their stories in later chapters. First, it's important that we make a few distinctions that will help us discern the difference between a movie's form and its message.

DIRECT VS. INDIRECT COMMUNICATION

As Jesus Himself knew full well and demonstrated in His parables, good storytelling communicates a message subtly and indirectly. Robert McKee puts it this way: "Audiences are rarely interested, and certainly never convinced, when forced to listen to the discussion of ideas."[10] What audiences want instead is to be hooked by a powerful story and engaging characters. When that happens, they are much more likely to hear a moviemaker's message and take it to heart.

Because audiences watch a movie primarily for its story, they can be extremely resistant to movies that forcefully promote a message with the intent to persuade rather than entertain them. People call this sort of movie "propaganda." The more blatant the message, the more likely it is to be taken as propaganda. For example, see if you can guess the message that is communicated in this quotation:

JACK: | *"Global warming is melting the polar ice caps and disrupting this flow. Eventually it will shut down. And when that occurs, there goes our warm climate.... If we do not act soon, it is our children and grandchildren who will have to pay the price."*

(The Day After Tomorrow)

Not very subtle, is it? Based on this short excerpt, the clear purpose of this film is to propagate a message about environmentalism. In contrast to this approach, storytelling techniques that communicate indirectly are more likely to capture the imagination of an audience and influence its ways of thinking. An excellent example of an indirect approach to the same topic addressed in *The Day After Tomorrow* is *WALL-E* (2008). This movie warns against pollution and human excess by following the daily experiences of a lovable character as he works to clean a wasted, garbage-strewn earth.

This raises the question of the purpose of movies. If the purpose is primarily to entertain, then a blatant message will come across as propaganda, and propaganda is only entertaining to those who already agree with the movie's message (consider, for example, the eager reception of 2004's *Fahrenheit 9/11* by those on the political left or 2008's *Expelled* by proponents of Intelligent Design). Almost by definition, then, popular movies will rarely state their messages explicitly. This means that determining what a movie has to say will probably require some investigation.

This insight has implications for Christian filmmaking. Christians often think of movies made by other Christians as a potentially effective means of evangelism. Filmmakers and writers may believe that if they can present the gospel clearly and dramatically, non-Christians will be convinced and repent. But if audiences tend to label direct messages as propaganda, then it is likely that when the protagonist delivers a successful gospel presentation to the antagonist at the climax of a movie, Christians will be the only people in the theater who are applauding. By stating their message too explicitly, filmmakers can actually undermine the purpose of their movie—in this case, evangelism. As film producer Ralph Winter (of *X-Men* and *Fantastic Four* fame) once said, "We have to master the art of filmmaking and create a powerful story before we think about how we're going to put some kind of Christian message in the film."[11]

Ironically, sometimes secular movies have communicated moral themes more effectively than their Christian counterparts. For example, the 1995 film *Heat* was a fairly unique heist movie for its time. The head of the *Heat* crew lives alone in a beautiful but barren house (an apt metaphor for his life, the guiding principle of which is reflected in his line below). His lieutenant has a gambling addiction and abuses his wife, who in turn cheats on him. The other crewmembers have all spent time in and out of prison and are merciless murderers. In *Heat*, being a criminal is not glamorous; it is a dark, hard life that is full of disappointments.

NEIL: | *"Have no attachments. Allow nothing to be in your life that you cannot walk out on in thirty seconds flat if you spot the heat around the corner."* (Heat)

The creators of *Heat* could have had one of the criminals get arrested, lose everything, meet a wise pastor while in prison, accept Christ, and end the film with a fiery sermon about the evils of crime. Instead this indirect, but clear, presentation of the emptiness of sin is much more powerful. We will return to this theme when we discuss questionable style elements (such as violence, profanity, and sexuality) in chapter 4.

DESCRIPTION VS. PRESCRIPTION

Filmmaker Lawrence Kasdan once said that "the thing about writing and directing a film is that you are presenting a view of the universe. . . . Every time you put the camera down you're saying here's a vision of the universe as I perceive it. And that is being tested by everyone who sees that movie."[12] This observation brings up another important distinction to bear in mind when evaluating the message of a movie. Just because a filmmaker communicates that something *is* the case does not necessarily mean that he thinks it *should be* the case. This is the difference between *description* and *prescription*. A filmmaker may describe urban life as violent and dangerous. That doesn't mean that he wishes urban life was dangerous or that he is glorifying violence. One can portray something without promoting it. The opening scene of *Saving Private Ryan* (1998) graphically depicts the horrors of war, but it doesn't communicate that what the world needs is more wars.

Readers of the Bible will recognize the truth of this principle immediately. Critics of the Bible will often point out how much violence and immorality is "in the Bible." However, the Bible does not affirm all the behaviors it records. It contains descriptions of murder, rape, drunkenness, and illicit sexual activity. But these are not prescriptions; the Bible is not saying that these things should have occurred, only that they did. Christians should remember this distinction when criticizing movies that simply portray immoral behavior. If immorality is portrayed as immorality, that is actually a good thing (Isaiah 5:20). This does not excuse gratuitous depictions or exploitation of such things, but it does mean we should allow for the communication of moral messages against immoral backgrounds.

MESSAGE VS. PURPOSE

A final distinction we should be careful to make when assessing movies is between the message and its purpose. We should avoid the temptation to assign motive to moviemakers based on the message of their movie. There are several important reasons for this.

First, if we incorrectly judge a filmmaker's motives based on certain elements of her film, we risk slandering the filmmaker. Consider accusations against Mel Gibson when he released *The Passion of the Christ* (2004). Because he (correctly) depicted the murder of Jesus Christ as being caused in great part by certain Jewish people of the first century, Gibson was accused of being anti-Semitic. Regardless of Gibson's personal thoughts on the Jewish people, simply telling this part of the story as it is recorded in Scripture[13] is hardly grounds for the charge of anti-Semitism.[14]

A second reason to avoid assigning motive is that films are rarely the creation of a single person. It is not unusual for a script to be written by one person, who then sells it to a studio, which has someone else rewrite it, only to hand it over to a director who can also change it. The director's power to influence the story may also be extended to the actors, who shape the work as well. After the filming is complete, changes to the story will often continue to be made in editing (thus the reason for "Director's Cut" versions of many movies). In fact, it is so rare for one person to receive singular credit for a film that the industry reserves a term for people who do: *auteur*. An *auteur* is a director whose influence is so strong in the films he directs that he is essentially considered to be its creator. Conversely, there is an option in place for directors who feel that they have lost control of a project so that they may choose to receive no credit for it.[15]

A final reason we should be slow to judge a moviemaker's motive based on the message of his or her movie is that sometimes a movie may communicate a message the creator did not intend.[16] In fact, there are times when a movie's indirect (and unintended) message overshadows the creator's direct (intended) message. An example of this is the 2006 film *Facing the Giants*. The movie's direct message is that we must trust and glorify God regardless of what happens in our lives. This is stated by various characters enough times that it's unmistakable. The clear theme of the movie is that we ought to give our concerns up to God, because we should desire His will above our own. However, in the course of the movie, no one faces disappointment with any of God's decisions, because every character trusts God and ultimately gets what he or she wanted in the first place! The indirect message of the film comes through loud and clear: a life lived for God gets you what you want. This unbiblical message might not be what the filmmakers had in mind, but it is what their story communicates.

So, when evaluating a movie's message, we should not necessarily be concerned over who is responsible for its creation or what their goal might have been when they made it. *The Lord of the Rings* trilogy (2001-2003) was not a product of Christian screenwriting, directing, or acting; yet, it is one of the most truth-filled stories ever to be shown on-screen. And this is not ultimately because it was based on books written by a Christian; it is because of the strength of the story itself.

CONCLUSION

All this is to say that when we set out to evaluate a movie's message objectively, we must let the story tell itself. As was the case with the parables Jesus told, stories come with their own guidelines for understanding the messages they carry. We ignore these guidelines when we fail to make the distinctions we discussed above. In the upcoming chapters we'll consider how stories are put together, how the different styles in which stories may be told impact audiences differently, and what role background plays in strengthening a story. Finally, in chapter 6, we will see how these elements combine into a coherent message. All of these things will help make you a better movie watcher and will make movies a lot more fun to watch.

REFLECTION QUESTIONS

1. Does the inclusion of a religious message in a film make it propaganda?

2. The Bible describes a lot of bad things (for example, violence and immorality). Why isn't this considered bad by most people?

3. If someone did not mean for a message to come through in a film, or meant for a different message to be communicated, does that change what message the film actually sends?

Story:
Structure, Sights, and Sounds

STORY RULES

KID:	*"You read that wrong. She doesn't marry Humperdinck, she marries Westley. I'm just sure of it. After all that Westley did for her, if she didn't marry him, it wouldn't be fair."*
GRANDPA:	*"Well, who says life is fair? Where is that written? Life isn't always fair."*
KID:	*"I'm telling you you're messing up the story, now get it right!"* (The Princess Bride)

It has long been recognized that there are certain elements that are common to nearly all stories. Almost intuitively, we can sense what should happen next in a story, how it should develop, or, at the very least, when something happens that seems out of place. When storytellers ignore these elements, listeners take notice. After all, it is his grandpa's breaking of these rules of storytelling that makes the grandson in *The Princess Bride* (1987) interrupt indignantly, "You're messing up the story!" As a form of storytelling, movies follow these same conventions of form and structure to develop their stories.

In addition to the nearly universal elements of the story, moviemakers use a variety of artistic techniques to articulate their message and enhance the viewing experience. Lighting, depth of focus, scene cuts, sound tracks, and many other cinematic devices change the way viewers experience the world of the film.

Understanding the basic elements of stories and being sensitive to the techniques moviemakers use to tell their stories is foundational to assessing the success of a movie.

STORY STRUCTURE AND CHARACTERS

Over two millennia ago, Aristotle pointed out the unique functions of the beginning, middle, and end of a story, what we'll call Acts One, Two, and Three.[17] In his landmark book *Screenplay*, Syd Field used this three-act structure to teach script writing, and this technique has been followed ever since.[18]

In this structure, each act has its own purpose, and each is separated by some story event. Moreover, character development is related directly to the form of the story. In other words, stories and characters develop (for the most part) along established patterns.

The purpose of Act One is to set up the story by introducing viewers to the main characters and telling them something about their situation. In technical terms, the "protagonist" is the main character, the one whom the action follows and with whom the audience is to identify in some way, and the "antagonist" challenges the protagonist and drives the conflict of the story. These are sometimes called the "hero" and "villain" respectively, but these more specific terms are not always accurate. Many times the protagonist is not terribly heroic, and antagonists are not always villainous. In fact, these characters aren't always even human. In the movie *Cast Away* (2000), the island served as the antagonist to the stranded human protagonist.

At some point after the setup, the time comes to discover what the story is really about. Once the characters are in place and their situation is known, some sort of challenge or conflict will arise. At this point in the story, the characters must choose how to face their challenge. Once that decision is made, the story pivots and starts in a new direction. This serves as the signal that the story has progressed into Act Two. In a typical movie, this usually happens near the half-hour mark.

The characters confront their challenge in Act Two. They overcome obstacles, make sacrifices, and face dangers. In other words, Act Two is where the action is. Consequently, Act Two also constitutes the bulk of a story, usually more than half. Regardless of how many twists and turns there are in this act, it is not over until one of two things happens: either the protagonist overcomes the challenge, or he is overcome by it. There are formal designations for these outcomes. In classical terms, a comedy is a story in which the protagonist meets and overcomes the challenge. In a tragedy the challenge is not met, and the protagonist is overcome by it. Either way, Act Two is not over until the climax. The *climax* resolves the challenge of Act Two and serves as the pivot point that separates Act Two from Act Three.

The purpose of Act Three is to show the final results of the climax. This is sometimes referred to as the *dénouement*. By this point, the viewer is fairly confident how the movie will end; now we will learn the final outcome of the story and the lasting effects of the climax. This act may be quite short. In some movies, Act Three is relegated to a single closing shot in which the credits begin to roll. In others, there may be a brief narration akin to an epilogue in a book.

THREE-ACT STRUCTURE

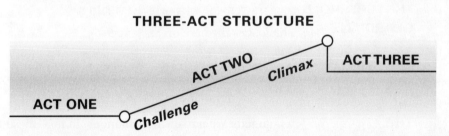

So, in "proper terminology," a story might read something like this generic fairy tale:

Once upon a time in Act One, there lived a protagonist. Things were going great until Act Two, when an antagonist came along and presented the protagonist with a challenge. The protagonist later realized that certain actions would have to be taken to meet the challenge.

At the climax, the protagonist overcame the antagonist's challenge, entered Act Three, and lived happily ever after.

The nice thing about these story elements is that they are objective and universal. It is not possible to tell a genuine story without a beginning, middle, and end. Moreover, these story elements are not simply a story-writing formula; Robert McKee writes, "Classical design is a mirror of the human mind."[19] These common story elements are so pervasive that myth researcher Joseph Campbell came to believe that all stories share the same basic features and conform to one universal pattern, what he called "The Hero's Journey."[20] Christopher Vogler, an accomplished screenwriter and Hollywood story consultant, divides the classic three-act structure into twelve stages wherein certain archetypal characters are used to move the story along and provide standard story functions:

THE HERO:	the protagonist, the main character whose actions form the story.
THE MENTOR:	the "wise old man" who supports the hero, often with a gift of some sort.
THE THRESHOLD GUARDIAN:	a character who supports the villain or challenges the hero on his journey.
THE HERALD:	a character who initiates the hero's call to adventure
THE SHAPESHIFTER:	a character whose function changes throughout the story.
THE SHADOW:	the villain, or the dark side of another character—even the hero.
THE TRICKSTER:	often a sidekick or minor character used for comic relief.

Vogler's twelve stages also reflect the classic three-act structure:

ACT ONE: *Heroes* are introduced in the *ordinary world*, where they *receive the call to adventure* by a *herald*. They are *reluctant* at first or *refuse the call*, but are encouraged by a *gift-giving mentor* to overcome the *threshold guardian* and *cross the first threshold* and *enter the special world*.

ACT TWO: Here they encounter *tests, allies, and enemies*. They approach the *inmost cave*, crossing a *second threshold* where they endure the *ordeal*.

CLIMAX: They take possession of their *reward* and are pursued on the road back to the *ordinary world*.

ACT THREE: They cross the *third threshold*, experience a *resurrection*, and are *transformed* by the experience. They *return with the elixir*, boon, or treasure to benefit the ordinary world.[21]

Later we will discuss how to use these observations to interpret and assess the movies we watch. For now it is enough to recognize these common story features when we see them. Fortunately, this task is often made simpler by film techniques that communicate meaning quickly through what we might call "film language."

FILM LANGUAGE: SIGHTS AND SOUNDS
Sights

My father used to drive me crazy, because he could almost always guess the end of a movie by midway through. When I asked him how he did it, he explained that everything in a movie has a purpose, so if you pay attention to what the movie shows you in the beginning, you'll often be able to guess what's going to happen at the end. He was right. Almost nothing in a movie is there by accident. What you see on the screen is very carefully controlled. What my father was referring to specifically is a principle of theater known as Chekhov's Gun. Anton Chekhov was a nineteenth-century playwright who said that if you show a gun in Act One, it had better be fired by Act Three.[22] In other words, show the audience nothing that is not important to the story. What this means to us is that every dominant element in a film, from what we see to what we hear, should matter.

This brings up our next film term: *mis-en-scene* (to impress your friends, pronounce it mee-zahn-sen with an *outrageous* French accent!). This phrase is used regularly in film analysis and literally translates as "put on stage." It refers to whatever is on the screen during a given shot, including physical scenery and the techniques used to present them.[23] Thus, mis-en-scene can include actors, sets, props, costumes, lighting, camera angles, lens focus lengths, aspect ratios, editing, and even the chemical treatments used to develop the film.

Because these elements help tell the film's story, it is a good idea to ask yourself why the filmmakers make the decisions they do. Note which actors are most or least attractive and which are the good guys and bad guys. Be alert to whether the scenes are shot in deep focus, presenting an overview and keeping viewers separated from the characters and action, or shallow focus, calling attention to certain objects or characters and creating intimacy. Identify which character the camera follows—is the scene shot from one character's point of view and do cuts follow their gaze? Are two scenes overlapped in a montage sequence, indicating parallelism in time or action? Do scene changes cut slowly (showing time's passage), do they cut rapidly (creating suspense), or is the scene one long take (creating gravitas)? Being sensitive to these techniques and others like them will not only increase your appreciation of the film but will also aid you in understanding what the filmmakers wanted to communicate.

A montage scene in *Pretty Woman* (1990), for example, shows the protagonist, Vivian, getting dressed. The scene consists of close-ups of various body parts and sexy clothing. This scene was not necessarily designed simply to arouse the audience. Rather, it establishes that Vivian, a prostitute, sees herself, and is seen by others, as just a collection of sexy body parts. To take another example, the famous introductory flyover of *Star Wars* (1977) begins with a tiny white transport vessel being pursued by an enormous dark battle-ship, brilliantly illustrating the impending struggle between a small band of good guys (the Rebellion) and the overwhelming enemy (the Empire). Finally, note the contrast between the dream world and the real world in *The Matrix* (1999). The dream world is shot in bleached-out, blue-green tones while the real world shows deeper, darker colors. These contrasting elements help the viewer to distinguish between what is supposed to be real and what is simply the false world of the Matrix.

Sounds

When I worked for a home theater retail chain, I used to show movies with the volume turned off in order to demonstrate how crucial a good sound system was to the overall impact of movie watching. It is not simply what we see but what we hear that helps us understand a movie's story. The sound, therefore, is just as carefully controlled in a film as the mis-en-scene. It is so important, in fact, that virtually everything we hear in a movie besides the dialogue—from the film's score to the actors' footsteps—is usually created in post-production. Again, almost nothing in a movie is accidental.

Diegesis refers to the sounds that come from the world of the movie. These could be external (car horns, dialogue, thunder) or internal (a narration in a character's mind). Even in subtle scenes such as the conversation in *The Patriot* (2000) in which Gabriel Martin confesses to his father that he would not return to open battle, the cannon fire in the background subtly reinforces Gabriel's concerns.

A film's score also communicates story by moving the emotions and creating mood. The intensity of the background music helps us to feel the mood of the scene. Imagine the funeral scene from *Braveheart* (1995) without the beautiful bagpipes playing in the background or the dénouement of *Titanic* (1997) without Celine Dion's "My Heart Will Go On." A film's score helps produce the emotional experience the director wishes to communicate.

Sometimes the score can also aid in narration and character identification.

This technique is known as *leitmotif.* A good example of this can be found in *The Lord of the Rings: The Fellowship of the Ring* (2001). For this film, themes were specifically written to provide proper atmosphere for characters and places. Hobbits, orcs, dwarves, and elves each had their own music, which mixed when the Fellowship arrived in Rivendell. Likewise, locations such as Moria, Mordor, and Hobbiton had distinctive sounds. In the realm of the elves, the music is light and beautiful (if a bit melancholy). Scenes involving the orcs showcase discordant "instrumentation" created with anvils and piano strings struck by chains.

Even the film's plotline was subtly revealed in its music. The first time we hear the Fellowship theme is when Sam steps dramatically into the cornfield—a step that takes him farther from home than he has ever been. This is the true beginning of the Fellowship, albeit with only two members (thus the simple instrumentation). When we hear the theme again at the conclusion of the council of Rivendell, it is fully orchestrated, because the Fellowship is now complete. The last time we hear it is when Frodo stands alone at the edge of the river above the falls, the sparse instrumentation confirming that the Fellowship has crumbled.

Leitmotif may also highlight a recurring theme (idea, person, or situation) with an associated melodic phrase or figure. In both the Broadway play and the film version of *The Phantom of the Opera* (2004), music is used to accentuate characters and actions. When we hear the initial chord blast from the pipe organ we know trouble is near! Because the song "Angel of Music" plays in scenes between Christine and the Phantom, and the songs "Think of Me" and "All I Ask of You" refer to Raoul and Christine's relationship, the mixing of these songs in "Point of No Return" in the final scene greatly intensifies the climactic clash of the three parties.

CONCLUSION

Being alert to these elements does not make objective assessment of movies a foolproof procedure. After all, despite a century of investigation, the art of movie making is still that—an art, with features open to interpretation and elements that are sometimes difficult to explain. Nevertheless, being equipped with a basic knowledge of the standard elements of a story and aware of the artistic techniques moviemakers use to tell their stories will help us avoid misunderstanding the messages of filmmakers. Be encouraged! We are well on our way to becoming faithful and confident movie watchers.

REFLECTION QUESTIONS

1. Think of one of your favorite movies and consider: Who is the protagonist? How are you supposed to identify with him or her? Who (or what) is the antagonist? Is the protagonist morally good? Is the antagonist morally bad?

2. Watch a familiar scene from a film and focus on everything except the main actors. How does the background contribute to what is being communicated?

3. Watch a familiar scene from a film with the sound muted and the subtitles on. What is the difference in your experience of the scene compared to when the sound is audible?

CHAPTER Four

Style:
How the Story Moves

THE VEHICLE VS. THE DESTINATION

As we discussed in the previous chapters, when evaluating the content of films, Christians need to avoid confusing message and method. In chapter 3, we explored various artistic techniques that moviemakers employ to tell their stories more effectively. Now we need to address style elements. There are many elements that we could consider, but this chapter focuses primarily on the use of profanity, violence, nudity, and sexuality, because these are the elements with which Christians are often most concerned.

I propose that style elements can be evaluated according to both their presence and their propriety. As we will see, the mere presence of profanity, violence, or nudity does not automatically indicate that a film is immoral as a whole. Whether their presence is acceptable in a film depends, in my view, on whether these elements support the story, or if they are merely gratuitous additions included to excite the audience.

BIBLICAL VS. CULTURAL MORALITY

When we critique a film's style elements we should do so from a biblical—rather than cultural—perspective. This is particulary true when it comes to profanity, sex, and violence. We must be careful not to make the mistake of assuming that our contemporary cultural judgments about what is biblically acceptable are always correct.

For instance, when the theologian-poet Dante Alighieri wrote *The Inferno*, he placed the lustful at the top ring of Hell and the violent closer to the bottom. This comes as a surprise to many Americans because so many of us have been conditioned to think that sexual sin is more immoral than violence. It is an established fact that Americans are far more concerned about sexuality and nudity in movies than violence.[24] In Europe, the opposite is true, and violence is taken much more seriously when rating a film. To judge these elements fairly, then, we must first consider what the Bible has to say about them.

Before we look into these issues in more detail, a word of caution is in order. Even when these style elements might be judged as appropriate to a film, the Christian must ask himself whether or not he should watch the film in the first place. While our subjective experience of a movie's style elements should not be the sole criterion in evaluating a film's overall goodness, we may need to avoid certain films simply because the style elements overshadow whatever good might be found in the film.

THE RATINGS GAME

Many Christians evaluate movies based primarily upon the Motion Picture Association of America (MPAA) ratings system. They might decide as a matter of principle, for example, not to watch any R-rated movies. Unfortunately, movie ratings do not necessarily provide an accurate evaluation of a movie's overall moral value. Whether or not a movie is moral depends upon an evaluation of both its message and its methods, and the ratings system largely overlooks messages.

Let's experiment. Based on the following descriptions, determine which of these movies is "better" from a moral perspective. Movie A contains profanity, nudity, and disturbing images of violence. Movie B is a family friendly cartoon with no nudity, cursing, or violence. Given these details, the answer might seem clear. But notice that all I gave you were style elements. If I add the following information, the equation changes: Movie A depicts history accurately, is anti-racist in message, and promotes conservative religious values; Movie B is dishonest in its presentation of history and anti-Christian in its message. The two films I am speaking of are the R-rated *Schindler's List* (Movie A) and

Disney's G-rated *Pocahontas* (Movie B).

It is important, then, that we understand what the rating system is intended to indicate. The MPAA ratings are designed to make adults aware of thematic elements that might be inappropriate for children. It is not intended to determine what makes for appropriate viewing for adults. Movies that are decidedly off limits for children are not necessarily inappropriate for the more mature.[25]

A student once asked me if I would let a two-year-old watch *The Passion of the Christ* (2004). I answered in the negative; but I added that I also would not feed a two-month-old infant a steak. Because she doesn't have any teeth, a two-month-old would probably choke on the steak. This is not because steak is deadly, but simply because a two-month-old is not developmentally ready to ingest it. It is often the same with movies.

I should clarify at this point that I am not suggesting that every R-rated movie is appropriate for adults. There are plenty of movies full of offensive style elements and devoid of a positive moral message. I am arguing only that the rating system is not a sufficient guide for making moral decisions about which movies to watch and which ones to avoid.

You may wonder why Hollywood can't just keep their films clean. Some people assume that all producers care about is making money and giving audiences what they indicate they want through ticket sales. This isn't necessarily true. Family-oriented films consistently turn greater profits in ticket sales than R-rated pictures. In fact, "by almost every measure, R-rated films are less likely to succeed at the box office than their G, PG, and PG-13 counterparts."[26] At the time of this writing, the only R-rated film in the top thirty all-time box office successes was *The Passion of the Christ*.

Part of the reason Hollywood continues to produce movies with these questionable artistic elements may be because of the ratings system itself. Because the MPAA bases its designations on appropriateness for children, audiences often think of G- and PG-rated films as kid movies. Thus, if a studio plans to make a "serious movie," it may push for an R rating in order to attract more adults.[27] (There are times, too, when producers eliminate some style elements to earn a lower rating, in order to attract younger viewers.) Because style elements change the ratings, the only way to attain an R rating is to include "adult elements." Further, filmmakers seeking peer applause and critical acclaim won't necessarily be concerned about either ticket sales or the public's taste. Movies that lack an "adult" edge might not attract the attention of critics the producers wish to impress. Unfortunately, this often means that many of Hollywood's best films will include style elements we might wish they didn't.

What this all boils down to is that Christians need to learn to exercise greater discernment in their movie choices. In one of its ratings explanation posters, the MPAA recommends that parents "think before taking the kids" when a film is rated R. I agree. I would add that regardless of rating, we should *always* think before we see a movie. The following sections will help us do just that by considering the three style elements mentioned above that are of particular importance to Christian moviegoers.

MPAA Ratings Explanation Poster[28]

PROFANITY / HARSH LANGUAGE

JUDGE:	*"Tell the witness to rephrase the answer."*
DEFENSE:	*"Well, that's just it, Your Honor. He can't. The word has a very distinct connotation. There's nothing else that quite captures it."*
PROSECUTION:	*"I object! You're saying the president of a bank can't articulate his thoughts without using profanity."*
DEFENSE:	*"What I am saying, sir, is that there aren't many words to describe the particular slime that your client oozes."* (From the Hip)

The late comedian George Carlin got a lot of mileage from his famous "Seven Words You Can't Say on TV" routine. He noted that "there are four hundred thousand words in the English language, and seven of them you can't say on television." While Carlin's math may be outdated, profanity in media continues to be a contested issue.

What is it exactly that makes a word profane? It can't simply be its definition. Some of the most common profanity concerns body parts and functions, sexual activities, or religious references that can be replaced with acceptable synonyms. That is, it seems it's not what a word means that makes it profanity, but the manner in which it is used. Looking closer, it seems that profanity is often a perversion of goodness (speaking of a good thing as if it were evil). This alone should give people pause when deciding how to express themselves. For the Christian there seems to be an additional issue, since the Bible also says to avoid the use of "harsh language."[29] This would clearly include many uses of profanity.

This warning does not, however, extend to merely impolite word choice.[30] Biblical writers used impolite language themselves at times, although it is often softened by less-than-literal translations. One famous example concerns

Paul's description of his former "good works" apart from Christ (Philippians 3:8) as *skubalon*, which means "rubbish or dung." It is easy to imagine how this might be translated in a less sensitive cultural environment!

The Old Testament contains many similar examples of impolite language. In Isaiah 64:6, the prophet compares Israel's righteousness to bloody menstrual cloths in contrast to God's righteousness. Men are described as those who "pisseth against the wall" (1 Samuel 25:22 KJV). Elijah sarcastically mocks the prophets of Baal by suggesting that their god is off "relieving himself" (1 Kings 18:27), and doomed men are described as those who will eat their own dung and drink their own urine (2 Kings 18:27). Israel and Judah are described as prostitute sisters who had their breasts "pressed and bruised" from handling (Ezekiel 23:3 KJV). Paul says he wishes that legalistic circumcisers would castrate themselves (Galatians 5:4-12).

In none of these cases was this sort of impolite language required simply to get the facts across. Such language was necessary to communicate the fullness of the writer's feelings and, perhaps, to shock listeners to attention. However it is explained, the same God who inspired Paul to write Colossians 3:8 ("put aside abusive speech" NASB) inspired these writers as well. So we should not judge something as immoral simply because it uses impolite language.

Strong profanity is another issue, and I think it is safe to conclude that Christians ought to avoid using it. However, in order to maintain realism and relevance, it may be argued that profanity is useful in some movies. Powerful films like *Schindler's List* (1993) or *American History X* (1998) would be laughable if the characters shouted "Gee whiz!" when confronted with violent, life-altering events. It is the gritty portrayal of the darker side of life that often causes Hollywood's unpopularity among Christian viewers, but it is the idyllic and unrealistic portrayal of life in some Christian movies that can make them ineffective in reaching unbelievers with a positive message.

So the presence of profanity in some movies should not automatically exclude them from consideration as otherwise moral films. We must always take context into consideration. It is good to show bad things as bad and good things as good. So if profanity (a bad thing) is celebrated, then criticism is appropriate; but we should take into account the fact that a character might use profanity in order to be realistic or to accurately convey the kind of person he or she is supposed to be. As with all potentially objectionable style elements, whether or not such usage justifies an individual's watching it for entertainment is a different question.

VIOLENCE

It would be difficult to define *the* Christian view on violence as believers hold a wide spectrum of opinions on this issue. I think this is because the biblical view of violence is that sometimes it is right and sometimes it is wrong. God has ordained appropriate violence in order to uphold justice, including actions ranging from capital punishment to war.[31] Jesus Himself was aggressive on occasion, as when He overturned tables and chased the moneychangers from the temple with a whip (John 2:14-15). Paul expected and accepted protection from the violent Roman army.[32] The common theme appears to be that God has at times allowed or commanded violence when it is used to protect the innocent or judge the wicked.

If violence is not always wrong, then it follows that its portrayal in movies is not always wrong. Just as in life, there may be instances when violence is more appropriate to a movie than non-violence. Consider *The Passion of the Christ* (2004). Some Christians took issue with the film's overly stylized violence while I found its visceral shock quite appropriate in a portrayal of Christ's sufferings.[33] Part of the problem, as I see it, is that evangelicals have historically downplayed the passion of Jesus. Yet Isaiah 52-53 indicates that Jesus was so brutalized that He was barely recognizable as a human, illustrating how ugly, distorted, and horrific sin truly is to God. *The Passion of the Christ* is effective in portraying the profundity of sin.

Ironically, although the quantity of violence in film is relatively high compared to everyday life, the realistic quality of it is rather low. The realistic consequences of violent activity are often toned down for movie audiences.[34] While this may seem like a positive practice, toning down violence to make it palatable may actually be more harmful than representing it accurately. Unrealistic violence can glorify violence or make it look like harmless fun. Compare the gun battles of *The Matrix* (1999) to the opening scene of *Sav-*

ing Private Ryan (1998), which gave viewers one of Hollywood's first realistic portrayals of the horror of warfare. It is easy to leave *The Matrix* wishing you could experience life like Neo, the film's protagonist. No one leaves *Saving Private Ryan* eager to experience war.

NUDITY / SEXUALITY

According to the Bible, nudity and sexuality are natural and good in their proper contexts. God's greatest work of art is mankind, and He made them naked. It was only after they had sinned and their relational intimacy was broken that they began to use clothing.[35]

While the presence of nudity in fine art is generally accepted, the issue of nudity and sexuality in movies is a bit more complicated.[36] The Bible is clear that sexual desire, when expressed in marriage, is healthy and beautiful (Song of Solomon; 1 Corinthians 7). The human longing for sexual intimacy is entirely appropriate. It stands to reason, then, that the portrayal of this longing on screen likewise can be entirely appropriate.

In fact, the Bible portrays appropriate sexuality in very descriptive, intimate language. If the Old Testament book Song of Solomon was read in a lot of churches today, many would be uncomfortable. So we see that in the context of the marriage relationship, the full breadth and beauty of sexual love can be expressed—and that artistic expressions that represent it in marriage can be appropriate.

While graphic and explicit portrayals of sex—even sex in marriage—should be considered out of bounds, there are tasteful means of portraying sexuality when warranted by the subject of the film. One need not put actions on display in order to communicate that they occurred.[37] Christians should also avoid the temptation to excuse sensual voyeurism in the name of art. Even in the Song of Solomon sexuality is a private matter not to be shared with onlookers (3:1; 5:4-6; 7:11-12). Further, if we have difficulty resisting temptations caused by certain film elements, then we should avoid them.[38]

Finally, we need to consider not only *whether* a movie depicts sexuality appropriately, but what claims it makes *about* sexuality. We should not celebrate any activity that the Bible condemns. According to Scripture, sinful sexual acts fall into two main categories: fornication, which is sexual activity between unmarried people, and adultery, which is sexual activity between married people and other partners.[39] It is also important to note that the Bible defines marriage as a relationship between two eligible humans of opposite gender.[40] So homosexuality, incest, bestiality, pedophilia, and other sexual perversions are not acceptable. Christians should never consider the positive depiction of sexual sin (whether graphic or not) as positive no matter how tastefully it is portrayed.

So, when evaluating films with sexual scenes, in addition to discerning whether or not the scene is gratuitous in nature, we should also be sure that we are evaluating the message communicated by the scene. Even fairly tame sexual scenes might send a bad message.

CONCLUSION

Unless immoral in the extreme, we should not automatically judge a movie as inappropriate based solely on its method of communication. Nor should we judge a movie as being good simply because we approve of its presentation. Rather, movies should always be evaluated on their treatment of a given subject and whether or not a film's style is appropriate. Style typically amplifies the message of a movie aesthetically or emotionally, so a movie's style should be in line with its significance (message).

Finally, we must avoid the common tendency to balk at offensive style elements in a movie while indiscriminately imbibing false worldviews and destructive philosophies when they are presented in non-offensive ways. People often drop their guard to view a G- or PG-rated film that might communicate a dangerously false message.

Next we will look at a film's suppositions, which are often difficult to distinguish from a movie's message.

REFLECTION QUESTIONS

1. What are the positive and negative aspects of deciding what movies to watch based on the MPAA ratings?

2. What should we do when we encounter something in a movie that we are uncomfortable with or feel guilty over?

3. Since our reactions to certain style elements differ, what approach should we take around others who are more sensitive than we are to movies or other activities? (See Romans 14 and 1 Corinthians 8.)

Suppositions:
The World of the Story

BEHIND THE SCENES

When the movie *Star Wars* was released in 1977, Christian reviews were mixed. Some critics attacked the movie for promoting Eastern religious ideals. Others called it a Christian allegory, one commentator going so far as to say that "the gospel according to Luke and the gospel according to [George] Lucas would seem to be virtually the same."[41] How could one movie spawn totally opposite reactions?

It seems that these critics disagreed over the influence of the worldview behind the story of *Star Wars*. As we will see in chapter 6, the message of a film is communicated primarily through the characters and what happens to them in the plot. These elements are not very difficult to discern, because they are in the foreground of the film, so to speak. However, the assumptions that form the backdrop for these characters can play an equally important role in determining a movie's message. We call these assumptions the "worldview" of the film—which isn't necessarily the same thing as its message. In fact, distinguishing the two is one of the more important, and difficult, tasks of evaluating movies.

WORLDS AND WORLDVIEWS

A worldview is the collection of beliefs or suppositions one has concerning the nature of reality. A film's suppositions are the collection of things it asks us to accept as true about the world in which its story takes place. These do not necessarily reflect the worldview of the filmmakers. The creators of *Reign of Fire* (2002), for example, likely do not believe that dragons will overtake the earth in the near future. Yet the world they created in the film presupposes the existence of dragons.

In order to enjoy a movie, an audience must be willing to temporarily accept the movie's suppositions. This is called "suspending disbelief." To suspend disbelief is to acknowledge that we are not expecting to be told the truth in every feature of the film. And there's nothing wrong with that—it's the nature of fiction. Even Jesus told parables about things that did not really happen. While the specific characters in a parable might not have existed, the stories communicated principles applicable to real life. And this was an accepted and acknowledged practice. Jesus was not being deceptive, nor did He falsify the actions of real persons. Suspension of disbelief lets the storyteller use fictional elements to communicate what is, hopefully, a true message.

This brings us, then, to our first lesson in discerning worldview: the type of fiction we're presented with influences how we understand a story's worldview. We might be tempted to assume that movies that are set in the "real world"—so that they suppose the things we suppose in real life—are intended to address real issues, while movies set in a fantasy world—or any place where the suppositions are different from daily reality—are meant only for entertainment. But this would be a mistake. This may explain why Dan Brown's *The Da Vinci Code* (film version 2006) caused such a stir in Christian circles, with its attack on traditional Christian beliefs. The film's fans could not understand why people would get so upset by a story everyone knew was fiction. The problem was that while the story was obviously fictional, it was played out against a realistic background, which made it seem like a revisionist history. By contrast, the 1998 film *Pleasantville* might be dismissed as pure fantasy because of its fanciful world of black and white. Yet the film provides a clear challenge to real world moral standards.

This brings up our second lesson in discerning worldview. Some background suppositions communicate a movie's message and some do not.

One very important aspect of film where this distinction plays out is genre conventions.

GENRE CONVENTIONS

Sometimes, a movie's suppositions have little bearing on the movie's overall message. This is often because of genre conventions. A genre is a category of storytelling made up of certain attributes including background assumptions that have been repeated until they become part of a formula (and, if overused, become clichés). These genre formulas help to orient the viewer quickly to the world of the film so as to avoid confusion and time-consuming exposition. We do not need to be told in a science fiction film that aliens exist, or that monsters in horror movies rarely die easily, or that baguettes must be purchased in romance movies. These elements are just part of the formula and are thus less likely to communicate anything important about worldview suppositions.

In other cases, genre conventions can help us discern a story's overall message. Because genres follow certain patterns, they create expectations (whether conscious or unconscious) in the minds of the audience. How a movie treats conventional genre patterns often provides clues to its message. Below we will consider several common genre types and how the suppositions of each may affect the movie's message.

Romance

HARRY: | *"I came here tonight because when you realize you want to spend the rest of your life with somebody, you want the rest of your life to start as soon as possible."*

(When Harry Met Sally)

In a romance or love story, the challenge is of utmost importance. Once the "boy meets girl" in Act One, something (and often a series of things) will stand in the way of true love. This challenge will drive the action of the movie all the way through to its climax. Through this process, we can often detect the writer's suppositions concerning how he or she understands the nature of love, whether it be passion, fidelity, self-sacrifice, or something else. In most cases, the message of a romance film will be that love is worth the effort of overcoming whatever challenge threatened to prevent it (tradition, family, social status, etc.).

Since the "sexual revolution" of the 1970s, most romance films will include a sex scene. Sex has become a customary element of the romance genre. Because marriage is rarely the solution to the challenge in a romance, but is simply an Act Three result of overcoming the challenge, sexuality will often be introduced before it is morally appropriate according to biblical ethics. As we discussed in the previous chapter, unnecessary sexual content in a movie may rightly offend many Christians, but it may also prevent them from perceiving the intended message of the movie. Because many viewers see sex as *the* expression of romantic love, sex has become a sort of archetypical action to portray romantic love on the big screen.[42] What this means for our purposes is that sexuality in movies expresses a certain worldview—the way many people understand the reality of love. However, this does not mean that a movie is *about* sex or that its overall message is sexual. Of course if the message of the film equates sex and love, then we are justified in criticizing it for being shallow.

Western

WYATT EARP: | *"You called down the thunder, well now you've got it.... So run, you cur, run! And tell all the other curs the law's coming. You tell 'em I'm coming ... and Hell's coming with me!"*   (Tombstone)

In the good old days, Westerns were often basic morality tales of good versus evil. The stories were simple and easy to understand: the bad guys come to harm the innocent and a hero arises to fight them. In Westerns, then, the worldview was fairly consistent and fairly straightforward. It assumed that in the world there are competing forces of good and evil. And typically the messages in this genre were simple and positive: the good guys win.

This kind of simplicity did not ring true for viewers in the cynical 1970s and 1980s, and many Westerns since then have evolved into more sophisticated dramas. They retain the settings and basic characters, but now they include considerable depth that was missing from the Westerns of old. Generally speaking, though, the Western still reflects high moral standards like honor, justice, and protection of the innocent—even if these values are illustrated through morally imperfect people who gunsling and fistfight.

Action / Adventure

PROXIMO: | *"Ultimately, we're all dead men. Sadly, we cannot choose how; but, what we can decide is how we meet that end—in order that we are remembered as men."* (Gladiator)

Action movies might seem like nothing more than mindless excuses for violence and car chases—and many are just that. However, some action movies can communicate a profound message beneath high-octane adventure sequences.[43]

In even the most action-packed specimens, there is often more to the movies than blowing up bad guys. For instance, *how* the protagonist fights might reveal something about the movie's suppositions. In the highly stylized fighting of martial arts films such as *Crouching Tiger, Hidden Dragon* (2000) and *Hero* (2002), fighting styles are deeply interconnected with the characters' philosophies. Similarly, *what* the protagonist is fighting for will often reflect the film's message.

Comedy

GAIL:	*"What are you doing here?"*
FLETCH:	*"I ordered some lunch."*
GAIL:	*"You ordered it here?"*
FLETCH:	*"Well, I knew this is where my mouth would be."* (Fletch)

Comedies are supposed to be funny. This may seem obvious, but we must remember this fundamental fact when we evaluate movies in this genre. After all, humor can often clothe a serious message. A comedy can undermine its serious message if its tone becomes too somber.[44] For this reason, although comedies often address weighty and serious issues, they do so lightly. These movies shouldn't be criticized simply because they appear to make light of a serious issue. In fact, it is for just this reason that comedies provide an important service. Audiences seem to have greater sympathy for certain topics when they are addressed in a lighthearted manner rather than in a dark and serious tone.

The comedy *Juno* (2007), for example, championed life as it addressed the topics of teen pregnancy and abortion. Using disarming comedy to deal with this emotionally charged subject helped keep the audience in sympathy with the protagonist. Had this serious subject been treated more intensely it might have lost the audience. On the other hand, comedies that use humor to mock their subjects need to be judged accordingly (even in Hollywood, abortions are not often used for laughs).[45] So in a comedy we need to evaluate both what is being made light of and how. Serious messages can be couched in comedic deliveries, and these can come in both negative and positive tones depending on what they are communicating.

Science Fiction and Fantasy

CORNELIUS: | *"Beware the beast man, for he is the Devil's pawn. Alone among God's primates, he kills for sport or lust or greed. Yea, he will murder his brother to possess his brother's land. Let him not breed in great numbers, for he will make a desert of his home and yours. Shun him, for he is the harbinger of death."*

(Planet of the Apes)

When evaluating movies in the science fiction and fantasy genres, it is important to ask whether the suppositions reinforce the message or are merely "window dressing." For example, the Disney version of *Cinderella* (1950) includes some magical elements such as a fairy godmother and talking mice. It is highly unlikely, though, that the story intends to communicate that these creatures should be considered real. Rather, the fairy-tale genre allows for fantastical creatures and events; these elements are to be expected. They appear in the book and film versions of C. S. Lewis's *The Lion, the Witch and the Wardrobe.* And Lewis certainly wasn't promoting witchcraft. Simply including fictional characters or creatures does not necessarily communicate a non-biblical worldview.

In science-fiction genre films there is often speculation upon the effects of cultural, technological, and political factors in society. *Planet of the Apes* (1968), for example, is set in a future time when the great apes have evolved to the point that they now rule over human beings. This is a questionable scenario from a Christian perspective. However, if we accept the filmmaker's suppositions, we discover the powerful statement about human nature summarized in the quotation above. Sometimes a true message can be communicated quite effectively through fantasy.

Horror

EMILY: | *"People say that God is dead. But how can they think that if I show them the devil?"*   (The Exorcism of Emily Rose)

Horror is probably the genre least favored by Christians. This is due in part to the genre's style elements, which often include graphic violence. Even so, the genre can communicate messages in a powerful way that other genres cannot.

This is because typical horror movies are often quite moral in their suppositions. The heroes and the villains are obvious, which is helpful in a world that often thinks of evil in shades of gray. In most horror movies the hero is the most morally pure character. The wise-man figure in the slasher film parody *Scream* (1996) recognizes this and includes "the sin factor" in his rules for surviving a horror movie.

Further, in contrast to the humanistic view of the innate goodness of mankind, horror movies also have a unique ability to show the dark side of man. Famous monsters like werewolves and vampires, as well as specific characters like Dr. Jekyll and Mr. Hyde, capitalize on the idea of man's struggle with inner evil. Most serial killer films depict the villains not as crazed lunatics, but as perfectly rational, intelligent people (a slap in the face to those who think only mentally sick people do evil).

On the flip side, many horror movies make too much out of the power of evil. The elevation of evil to the point where goodness can just barely overcome it sends a poor message. It seems that good wins battles but never the war. While this can be attributed mostly to the desire for sequels, it may send a false message that evil can never be finally eradicated. Whether or not horror films can be justified on a theoretical basis, we must always be careful not to cross the line from enjoying a bit of scary fun to developing a fascination with evil.

Revisionist

Although background assumptions in genre-specific movies don't always communicate important worldview suppositions, we should always pay attention when a film "breaks the rules." Rejecting the formula in a given genre is known as "genre revisionism." The infamous film *Brokeback Mountain* (2005) was a rather startling example of revisionism in Westerns, with its use of homosexuals as the main characters. (This is evident even without watching the movie.) The less-than-perfect superheroes in *Iron Man* (2008) and *The Dark Knight* (2008) can be considered revisions of the hero character motif. In these cases, it may be instructive to ask why a filmmaker chose to work within a genre but broke the rules. He may simply be striving for originality. More likely, he may be questioning the common worldview suppositions that form the background for other films in that genre.

TEST CASE: HARRY, GANDALF, AND ASLAN

We have seen that when discerning a movie's worldview we must distinguish mere background elements from those important to the movie's message. This is not always easy, however. This can be illustrated by the debate over several fantasy-oriented films that, because they are in the same genre, can appear to share a worldview when, in fact, they do not.

In the late 1990s, the popular *Harry Potter* books became some of the best sellers of all time and were quickly made into movies. Many Christians expressed concern about the use of occult magic, witchcraft, and sorcery in the books and movies. They feared that children who watched the movies (or read the books) would be enticed into dabbling in the occult because of the way the stories glorify the dark arts.

A common counterargument offered by Christians and non-Christians alike was that these same elements are found in two Christian fiction classics, namely C. S. Lewis's *The Chronicles of Narnia* and J. R. R. Tolkien's *The Lord of the Rings*, which were also both made into movies. Both movies had magic and wizards. So why were these things bad for Harry but not for Gandalf? If magic and sorcery could be used in tales written by Christians, then why was *Harry Potter* author J. K. Rowling castigated for using them?[46] I suggest it's because the stories have differing worldview suppositions.

GANDALF: | *"There are many magic rings in this world, Bilbo Baggins, and none of them should be used lightly."*
(The Lord of the Rings: The Fellowship of the Ring)

The Lord of the Rings trilogy (2001–2003) takes place in a world of Tolkien's imagination called Middle-earth. Middle-earth is a fantasy world; a "sub-creation" where magic is part of the created order. In Middle-earth one finds nonhuman beings—orcs, dwarves, elves, and hobbits, to name a few— that can do things humans cannot. While the elves are probably the most obviously "magical" creatures in Middle-earth, there are other creatures that are far more powerful. Though it is not made clear in the film adaptations of the stories, Gandalf the Wizard is not human; he is a Maia. The Maiar are angelic beings in the service of the Valar, who are themselves cocreators with Eru-Ilúvatar, the creator-god of the universe. Thus Gandalf is not a wizard by the occult definition: he is not a human with magical powers. Magic for Gandalf is not unnatural or occultist. It is part of his nature. Magic for men and hobbits, however, is unnatural, and leads to their demise.

WHITE WITCH: | *"Have you forgotten the Deep Magic?"*

ASLAN: | *"Don't cite the Deep Magic to me, witch!*
I was there when it was written."
(The Chronicles of Narnia:
The Lion, the Witch and the Wardrobe)

That the events in The Chronicles of Narnia do not take place in our world is made perfectly clear in The Magician's Nephew (a book that has not yet been adapted for the screen). In this prequel to The Lion, the Witch and the Wardrobe, the main characters witness the creation of a world called

Narnia. In Narnia, Aslan, the Great Lion, has made a new world with all kinds of magical creatures in it. In a manner similar to *The Lord of the Rings*, this world has certain attributes that ours does not—including creatures with the ability to perform acts that would be impossible in our world. This is made all the more clear by the White Witch's inability to work magic when she enters our world. In other words, magic in both *The Lord of the Rings* and *The Chronicles of Narnia* is not equivalent to the occult practices in which people in the real world can be involved. When the Bible commands against the use of sorcery and divination, it is not referring to the magical things that magical creatures can do in fantasy worlds.

HAGRID:	*"If that dolt of a cousin of yours, Dudley, gets up to any mischief, you could always threaten him with a nice pair of ears, to go with that tail."*
HARRY:	*"But, Hagrid, we're not allowed to do magic outside Hogwarts. You know that."*
HAGRID:	*"I know that, but your cousin don't, do he?"*

(Harry Potter and the Sorcerer's Stone)

Harry Potter, it has been argued, is the opposite case. Instead of taking place in a fantasy world, the story unfolds in our world, as its author has admitted.[47] Magic in *Harry Potter* meets the definition of occult magic performed by human beings. Magic is considered a neutral power in *Harry Potter*, so evil uses of magic are countered by good uses, and "Muggles," humans who refuse to practice magic, are looked down upon as simpleminded.

Although these films all share certain fantasy suppositions, the differences in worldview between *The Lord of the Rings*, *The Chronicles of Narnia*, and *Harry Potter* are significant enough to warrant consideration when the messages of the movies are evaluated—especially in terms of how they represent the use of magic.[48] Whether or not these differences are sufficient to condemn the *Harry Potter* series, I will leave to the reader to consider. Here I simply wish to point out that the inclusion of similar elements is not always equivalent to similar suppositions.[49]

CONCLUSION

Along with style, background suppositions are part of the storytelling techniques that help us discern the message of a movie. Sometimes they are simply genre features. At other times they may form part of the message. In the next chapter, we'll see how these elements combine to create a complete movie experience.

REFLECTION QUESTIONS

1. How can a movie that takes place in a made-up world still tell a true story?

2. Is the real world the only world in which biblical morality matters?

3. Which movie genres can most effectively communicate biblical, moral themes? Why?

CHAPTER SIX

Significance:
The Moral of the Story

PUTTING IT ALL TOGETHER

As we have seen in previous chapters, stories have built-in mechanisms for communicating messages. By paying careful attention to these mechanisms, we are able to make objective interpretations and evaluations of movies.

We have also seen that a movie is made up of many elements: the story that the movie tells (chapter 3), the style used to tell the story (chapter 4), and the story's background or worldview suppositions (chapter 5). We have seen that the style of a movie is significant to the message, in that style elicits various emotional and aesthetic reactions (positive or negative) in the audience to amplify the story. We have also discussed how the background suppositions of a movie may simply serve as a backdrop to the story, highlight some feature of the story by breaking genre conventions, or figure prominently in the message. While all these elements can be important in the evaluation of a film, the significance (message) of a movie is primarily revealed through the movie's story structure and characters.

STORY

In chapter 3 we discussed story structure, including the elements and purposes of the individual acts. In a movie all of these elements should combine to tell one coherent story with a discernable message. As an aside, one cannot very well use a classical story structure (which assumes a purposeful, ordered reality) to assert a random, nihilistic worldview.[50] In this chapter we'll explore how all these things come together.

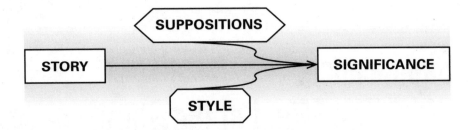

Act One: Characters and Convictions

In order to discern the message of a movie, it is important to pay attention to how Act One establishes a story's characters. Filmmakers often tell their audiences something significant about the characters by how they introduce them, by what they are doing when we first see them. Most of the film's suppositions will be revealed in Act One. So from the first time we meet a character, and as Act One progresses, we should ask ourselves such questions as: Who is the protagonist and who is the antagonist? Do the main characters have any obvious weaknesses or strengths? Do they express a particular ideology? The answers to these questions will aid us in discerning the writer's message. The protagonist is the character the audience is supposed to identify with, so this character is important to the writer's message. Thus it is helpful to note the protagonist's goal, what challenges he must face in reaching it, what decisions he must make in order to resolve the struggle, and the consequences of his final actions and decisions.

Once we've identified the main characters and have begun to get to know them, our next step is to identify other character types and the functions they serve at various points in the story. This will help us grasp how the story is moving along. As discussed in chapter 3, these other characters will play off of the protagonist in some fashion. Sometimes the relationships between main and secondary characters can communicate a lot about the film's worldview.[51] Going back to the Campbell/Vogler archetypes, for example, "mentors" will typically represent the same message as the protagonist, while "shadows" and "threshold guardians" will often oppose it. In a coherent story, the main characters will support the main message either negatively or positively.

Act Two: Challenges and Goals

While we are given some preliminary insight into the characters in Act One, we really get to know them as they begin to face the challenges of Act Two.

The challenge that separates Act One and Act Two will reveal something of value to the protagonist that is unattainable for some reason. This may be an object (like money or the Holy Grail), but it could also be something abstract, such as living in peace. The threat to that thing of value will drive the plot as the protagonist strives to possess it. The manner of this pursuit reveals something of the character of the protagonist, and the goal often changes as he meets challenges along the way. How the protagonist overcomes challenges (or succumbs to them) and how his goals change form the backbone of the story and help us understand what the filmmaker is trying to communicate.

For example, Act One might introduce a single woman desperately looking for a husband. We pivot into Act Two when her current boyfriend announces that he plans to leave the country to study abroad for a year. After deciding he is "the one," she spends the first half of Act Two trying to sabotage his plans. When each of her attempts is thwarted, she changes tactics and decides to make him jealous by pretending to date an ex-boyfriend. This new relationship, which begins as a farce, becomes more enjoyable with each of the staged dates. She comes to realize that, in her desperation, she had overlooked significant flaws in her current boyfriend—flaws that her fake date doesn't have. But her scheme works, and her boyfriend proposes marriage. Now she must choose between her real boyfriend and her fake love interest (who has become her real interest). This change of values will undoubtedly form the basis of the film's climax.

Assuming the writer follows the rules of a romance movie, we all know what she will do. She will choose the "fake" boyfriend and they will live happily ever after. The message of the movie will be that true love is more important than marrying the wrong person just to be married. However, the writer may break the rules and have her marry the wrong man. This should remind us that while Act Two normally sets us up for the message of the movie, we cannot be certain until the climax. It has been said that "a movie is its last twenty minutes." In other words, it is at the pivot from Act Two into Act Three that the message of a movie becomes clear. This pivot is known as the climax.

Act Three: Climax and Dénouement

Of all the story parts that drive the message, perhaps none is more important to consider than the climax. Up to this point, we do not know whether the protagonist's goals will be met, or how. We do not know if our hero will overcome her challenges or be defeated by them. In a (classic) comedy, remember, the hero overcomes the challenge of Act Two. Thus, in a comedy the message is communicated positively; it tells you what the screenwriter thinks is the case. Conversely, in a (classic) tragedy, the hero is overcome by the challenge. This can communicate the same message that a comedy can, only in negative terms.

For example, imagine a movie in which a young girl has parents who abuse drugs. She is challenged throughout the film with the temptation to adopt their lifestyle, but she ultimately overcomes by refusing. Thus at the climax, she may decidedly say "no" and go on to live a healthy, drug-free life. Now imagine another movie with the same basic premise. In this film, however, the girl fails her challenge, becomes addicted to drugs as well, and eventually dies from an overdose. Although the films told different stories, they send the same message: however great the temptation, resisting drug use is the wise choice. One movie celebrates the hero's good decision, while the other shows the results of a bad decision. A moviemaker's decision to follow one path or the other will likely depend upon the weight of the message. That is, while many people prefer a happy ending (a classic comedy), sometimes a message can be communicated more powerfully by a classic tragedy.

The final moments of Act Three, sometimes referred to as the *dénouement*, are when the story is finally wrapped up. The *dénouement* traces the events following the climax, tying up loose ends and giving the audience some idea of how things will go from here (or whether there will be a sequel!). What happens as a result of the climax can be an important key to understanding the movie's message. In the movie *Thirteen* (2003), we must wait until the last scene to see the final effects of a teenage girl's yearlong rebellion. We have already discovered the painful outcome of her actions at the climax, but we are not certain whether she will bounce back or lose it completely until the last second.

OTHER ELEMENTS

The message of a movie will be most clearly communicated through its characters and their actions during the story. These story elements can be augmented, highlighted, and amplified by the way the story is told (style) and by its worldview (suppositions).

Style

In chapter 4, I argued that a proper evaluation of a movie requires an eye for the difference between style and message. The inclusion of certain style elements and the way they are depicted can reinforce a movie's message.

In *Idiocracy* (2006), for example, people of the future have become so stupid and immoral that they can barely express themselves without cursing or making sexual innuendos. While Christian audiences might object to the frequent use of profanity and sexual references in the film, in the end, those elements are used to make a point that we might agree with!

The main thing to look for with regard to style when it comes to discerning the message of a movie, is how the style is used to amplify the story elements. A good question to ask is, "How else could this scene have been shot and what would that have changed about the characters/setting/etc.?" A movie's style should always appropriately reinforce the impact of its message. Otherwise, those style elements may be considered gratuitous.

As stated before, whether or not an individual should view films with certain potentially objectionable elements is another question. That answer will depend on personal conviction as well as the biblical considerations that will be discussed in the final chapter.

Suppositions

In chapter 5 we observed that a movie's suppositions can be central to its overall message in some cases and largely inconsequential in others. In order to evaluate a movie fairly and accurately, it is crucial that we determine how the movie's suppositions are related to its message.

The *X-Men* series (2000–2006), for example, is predicated upon, but does not promote, evolutionary theory. Evolution just serves as the background for explaining the mutant characters' powers. Perhaps the characters' gene alterations could have come about in a different way, like in *The Incredible Hulk* (2008) or *Spider-Man* (2002), but this would have been more difficult to explain on a worldwide scale. It also would have lessened the story's "cautionary tale" nature regarding who should be considered human. Although normal humans fear the mutants, it is the *villain* (Magneto) who wants non-mutants treated as inferior beings. Contrast this with the *X-Files* (1993) film, where we discover that aliens seeded earth to get human evolution going and then wrote the Bible to guide us. This revelation comes at the climax of the film where the skeptical character is shown to have been wrong. In *X-Files*, evolution is hardly a subtle background element!

The background suppositions in the 2005 film *The Exorcism of Emily Rose* caused some critics to misunderstand the movie's message. The story concerns a Catholic priest who is on trial for murder, because Emily Rose died while he was trying to exorcize her demons. Some Christian viewers became distracted by the film's portrayal of religious faith. They were so focused on whether or not believers could be demon-possessed or if the film was promoting Roman Catholic theology that they ultimately missed the point. But in this case both Roman Catholicism and the exorcism were simply part of the background. The story follows a courtroom drama, so it might seem that the priest and the jury's verdict are the keys to the movie's message, but I don't think so. The priest's lawyer is the only character to undergo serious change in the film, and the purpose of the climax is to reveal whether this skeptical lawyer can be objective enough to successfully argue for the possibility of the supernatural. That is to say, both the exorcism and the priest function as the background for the lawyer's struggle, which itself carries the message.

Or consider the philosophically interesting film series previously mentioned called *The Matrix*, which began in 1999. This film and its sequels (*Reloaded* and *Revolutions*) raised intriguing questions about human knowledge of reality as well as the question of free will. The films combined elements of Christianity, Buddhism, and postmodernism to serve the film's quasi-symbolic nature. Ultimately the films assume an Eastern mystical worldview. Although they contained certain Western or Judeo-Christian elements (especially the first film), the films represent classic Eastern thought (reincarnation, karma, Brahman) through the sci-fi genre. This becomes clear at the conclusion of the trilogy, when the hero and villain merge into each other and then back into the "source" in order to end the war of the machines.

PUTTING IT INTO PRACTICE

It will be helpful before we move on to put our tools of movie evaluation to work on an actual film. So, as an exercise in movie evaluation, let's look again at *Star Wars Episode IV: A New Hope* (1977). I stated above that the series had a decidedly Eastern worldview (although it tells an essentially Western story). Another theme emerges in *Episode IV* that is important to the series as a whole, as well as the perspective the movie wants us to adopt. That message becomes clear as we analyze the movie's story, style, and suppositions.

In Act One we meet the protagonist, Luke Skywalker. We first see him looking off into space in the stance of a heroic dreamer, and the film score is uplifting. He learns from Obi-Wan Kenobi (his mentor) that he has the Force. Obi-Wan gives Luke a light saber and teaches him the ways of the Force, after the young man receives a call to action from two droids (one a herald, the other a trickster). Luke is deterred from his dreams of joining the rebellion by his uncle (the threshold guardian) who knows of his ties to the Force. The villain is clearly Darth Vader (Luke's shadow).[52] His violent entrance into the movie, his dark suit, and the brooding death march that serves as his theme music combine to make it clear that he is the bad guy. Vader also believes in the Force, and he leads the evil Empire that opposes the Rebellion (and the hero).

In Act Two Luke decides to join the Rebellion. We meet Han Solo (a shapeshifter), who initially disagrees with Luke and Obi-Wan with regard to the Force. Together they rescue the damsel-in-distress, who has discovered how to stop the Empire. At the climax, Luke uses the Force to overcome the challenge of the Empire by destroying the Death Star.

Act Three ends with the good guys receiving their rewards and joining in a victory celebration. Obi-Wan dies (in a sense) and Darth Vader escapes, but these elements serve to set up the sequels. Together, these elements reinforce the film's one simple message: trust in the Force. The Force—which is activated by emptying the mind, controlling emotional states, and trusting intuition over rational thought—reflects classic Eastern or New Age mysticism. It is important to note that the actual non-existence of the Force in the real world is unimportant; what it represents in reality is what counts.

The *Star Wars* trilogy provides an interesting contrast to *The Matrix*. There is no question (based on statements made by creator George Lucas and the story itself) that the film assumes an Eastern worldview, as does *The Matrix*. The mystical Force, the energy-nature of all living beings, the subjective nature of truth—all of these elements illustrate an unquestionable adherence to Eastern thought. Interestingly, however, *Star Wars* ultimately followed a decidedly Western (and Judeo-Christian) story line: good triumphs over evil. Undoubtedly, this is part of the reason many moviegoers found this trilogy more satisfying than the *Matrix* movies. More importantly for our purposes, it illustrates how a movie's message is not bound to its suppositions.

THE BIG PICTURE: A FILM'S ULTIMATE SIGNIFICANCE

The message of a story, its overall significance, is more universal than its particular story. In order to get to the universal message of a movie, we need to abstract it from the story's particular features. This is usually a fairly intuitive process—in fact, kids do it all the time. When we tell the story of *Goldilocks and the Three Bears*, no kid thinks that the moral of the story is "don't steal porridge from bears and fall asleep in their bed." Rather, it is simply "don't steal." And probably no one saw the message of *Star Wars* as "people ought to own droids," or "battle station exhaust ports should be securely covered." These are just the particulars used to create the background suppositions and tell the story. The significance of *Star Wars*, or any movie, is greater than any of its parts.

Universal principles are communicated through characteristics or actions that are common to all people. If these are absent from a film it will fail. Why? Because our connection to the characters, particularly the protagonist, is what makes stories work. The only way, then, to make a popular film is to choose stories that feature characters who are dealing with universal issues.

Now, we won't all face death in the Roman Coliseum—but we will all face death. We won't all fight in a major world war—but we all have our battles to fight. We don't all set land speed records, meet space aliens, have super powers, sing in an opera, or start successful careers in country music—but there are themes in all of these experiences that we do share, because we have a common nature. Because we share some universal themes in all of our particular lives, we can all connect our life stories at a universal level. Moreover, this common ground can be useful in communicating the most important of all stories—the gospel. In the next section of the book, we will explore how the messages of a number of movies compare with the message of the gospel.

CONCLUSION

To summarize what we have discussed to this point, the distinctions between style, story, suppositions, and how they contribute to a film's over-all message (significance) are crucial for accurate movie interpretation and evaluation. Keeping these different facets before us can help us dispel distractions and let a movie speak for itself. Then we can fulfill our responsibility as moviegoers: to discover what a movie is saying about what it is portraying.

Christians should realize that the messages of movies, whether good or bad, can be useful launching points for spiritual discussions. Movies address an enormous range of themes. And while many of these are truly important (racism, drug abuse, love, loyalty, family), how Hollywood treats the subjects of truth, God, Scripture, and salvation is the most important of all.

In the chapters that follow, we will look at these themes—both how they have been approached and how well Hollywood has answered the questions they raise. We will consider how to discern what Hollywood is saying through the films it produces. And we will explore how to use Hollywood's messages (the good and the bad, the true and the false) as culturally interesting inroads for presenting, clarifying, and justifying the gospel.

REFLECTION QUESTIONS

1. Is it okay to watch movies that tell stories about evil? If not, why are so many stories about evil recorded in Scripture? If so, what are the dangers in watching such stories for entertainment?

2. Is it legitimate to read spiritual messages into a movie that go against what the movie actually communicates?

3. Is the gospel story a comedy or a tragedy (in their classic senses)? If it is a tragedy, did Jesus fail to overcome the challenge? If it is a comedy, how did Jesus overcome the challenge?

ACT TWO

EVALUATING & DISCUSSING MOVIES

DISCUSSING MOVIES RELIGIOUSLY:
Is Salvation Self-Realization or Sincere Repentance?

FAITH ON FILM

DARTH VADER: | *"I find your lack of faith disturbing."*

(Star Wars: A New Hope)

For all its alleged tolerance, Hollywood often portrays religion in a negative light.[53] This has not always been the case. During its "Golden Age," Hollywood positively portrayed religious figures in movies like *The Ten Commandments* (1956) and *Ben-Hur* (1959). And, to be fair, there have been several examples of religion-friendly films in recent years. Both *Bruce Almighty* (2003) and *Evan Almighty* (2007) succeeded as comedies without being abusive in their portrayal of God and faith. *The Addiction* (1995) raised some interesting issues about faith and morality. And that's not to mention explicitly religion-friendly films such as *The Chronicles of Narnia: The Lion, the Witch and the Wardrobe* (2005) and *Amazing Grace* (2006).

Nevertheless, these films are the exceptions that prove the rule. Many other movies feature fallen priests, ignorant believers, or just plain religious nuts. Like the archetypical "cop on the edge," the "distant father," or the "hot nerdy girl," these "crackpot Christian" characters have become staples of the movie industry.

What this means is that Hollywood rarely relieves the difficulties Christians face in trying to persuasively communicate our faith. Consider the ridiculous "Christians" of *Saved!* (2004). The plot revolves around a Christian girl who gets pregnant while trying to save her boyfriend from turning gay by giving up her virginity to him (because Jesus told her to, of course). In the meantime, her mother is having an affair with the pastor/principal of the local Christian high school, and her schoolmates are each discovering just how lame Christianity is. The clear message of the movie is that whatever anyone does is fine, so long as they follow their hearts, so we should all stop judging each other. Now, there's nothing wrong with a good lampoon, and we should be able to laugh at ourselves. But an entire cast of one-dimensional caricatures is little more than propaganda.

Besides developing characters like these that essentially function as Christian dupes, Hollywood has also produced decidedly anti-religious films such as *The Handmaid's Tale* (1990), which depicts a world in which women are used as sex-slave breeders in an America run by religious fanatics. *At Play in the Fields of the Lord* (1991) equates missionary work with cultural destruction. Other films like *The Last Temptation of Christ* (1988), *The Da Vinci Code* (2006), and *The Golden Compass* (2007) each cast a negative hue over religion in general or some important aspect of Christianity in particular.

These frontal assaults on religion pose serious threats to the popular perception of Christians. And that is no small thing. But there is another type of film message that can be more harmful still. Rather than attack the Christian faith directly, many films undermine foundational Christian principles, including the human need for salvation. These films present a false "gospel" that leads people away from the truth. Recognizing these messages in movies can help us avoid being adversely influenced by them. Just as importantly, the messages in these stories can provide us with starting points for sharing the true gospel of Jesus Christ.

A WAY THAT SEEMS RIGHT

CASANOVA: *"We're not evil because of the evil we do ... we do evil because we are evil."* (The Addiction)

One thing people find particularly offensive about Christianity is its teaching that people are inherently sinful and need to be saved by the God they are rebelling against. This is a crucial point, for without sin there is no need for salvation. That's why the apostle Paul spends the first three chapters of Romans discussing sin before he moves on to discuss the possibility of salvation.

Unfortunately, people don't like to think of themselves as sinful. They don't want to believe that they are selfish, evil people who would act much worse if unrestrained by society (as the 1990 film *The Lord of the Flies* or the 2000 film *The Beach* illustrated). Because they believe they act from pure motives, many people live by their own moral code and can always justify their behavior. When that strategy fails, they can always think of someone worse than themselves.

The popular view of ethics today is that morality is relative to the individual or to their culture. This is called moral relativism. Because people believe everyone should determine his or her own personal ethics, "tolerance" has become the new—and sometimes the only—universal virtue. You can imagine what the gospel sounds like to someone who claims to believe in moral relativism: not only are Christians judgmental, but they choose to follow a religion that punishes people for disobeying someone else's moral code!

The Addiction (1995) is a good example of a film that shows the problems of moral relativism. The main character is a graduate student, and a vampire, who is doing research in philosophy. She is concerned with the problem of evil (including her own). But her professors are unable to help her deal adequately with the issue, because they are committed to a relativistic worldview.

In contrast to this worldview, Christianity assumes moral absolutism. Moral absolutism relies on overarching moral principles that apply to all people. This position affirms that we are all born with a conscience; we all know instinctively when we have been wronged or when we have wronged others. We act as though we expect others to recognize this as well: we argue (not just fight) over right and wrong and expect others to honor the overarching law of basic right and wrong. Moreover, Christians derive their commitment to moral absolutism from Scripture. From the beginning, God communicated to human beings that some things were good and some were bad (Genesis 2–3), and even before the Ten Commandments, people recognized a universal moral code (Genesis 4). Paul points out in the book of Romans that there is a universal moral law that all people recognize (Romans 2).

Christians recognize that humans are in need of salvation because we know there is right and wrong and yet we often choose to do wrong. Because the Creator establishes moral standards, He is just and fair and punishes our sin. Fortunately for us, the same Bible that reveals our evil also offers us a way of redemption.

SALVATION STORIES

But it is not only Christians who recognize the need for salvation. Several story analysts have noted that salvation of some sort is a common theme in movies.[54] If that sounds surprising, it may be because many people, including some Christians, often think of salvation only in terms of the ultimate redemption from sin that is found when people put their faith in Jesus Christ. But Scripture uses the term more broadly. The Bible speaks, for example, of Israel's salvation from Egypt (Exodus 14:30), of armies from enemies (Joshua 10:6), and even of wheat from invaders (Judges 6:11)! The New Testament speaks of salvation in regard to drowning (Matthew 14:30), crucifixion (Luke 23:35; John 12:27), judgment (Acts 2:40), a storm (Acts 27:20, 31), Christian labor (1 Corinthians 3:15), a bad conscience (1 Peter 3:21), and childbirth (1 Timothy 2:15). So whenever we speak of salvation, we should always be sure we know who is being saved and from what.

Because of the narrative nature of movies, salvation—in this more generic sense—is virtually a necessity.[55] After all, stories are activated by conflict, and conflict has to be resolved in order to complete the story in a satisfying manner. Now, salvation in movies will almost never be salvation of the ultimate, eternal sort. But this does not diminish the importance of more limited stories of salvation.

Recall the importance of the climax from chapter 6. When it comes to movies, we can consider the conflict and climax as a film's "testimony," much as a Christian might recount his or her experience of salvation. The protagonist faces a challenge and will either be destroyed (tragedy) or redeemed (comedy). To some extent, therefore, movies all present either salvation gained or salvation lost. We can determine a movie's salvation message by considering how it answers the following questions:

ACT ONE: Who are we and where did we come from?

CONFLICT: What happened to mess it all up?

ACT TWO: What are the choices that we have to make to rectify the situation?

CLIMAX: What ultimate choice should we make?

ACT THREE: What are the consequences of our choice?

ROSE: | *"He saved me, in every way that a person can be saved."*

(Titanic)

ULTIMATE SELF-REALIZATION

Oftentimes in Hollywood films, salvation is understood as "self-realization." According to Maslow's Hierarchy of Needs, self-realization is the pinnacle of human experience, and films from *The Wizard of Oz* (1939) to *Rambo* (2008) reflect that idea. The 1998 film *Rounders* is a good example of this. The protagonist, Mike McDermott, is a professional poker player who has given up his love of the game to pursue a legitimate career in law.

Everything in the story argues against this choice: his best friend chides him for not doing what he does best; his mentor-professor calls it a mistake to ignore your true calling in life. Only his girlfriend demands that he give up gambling. In the end, he gives in to his true nature and wins big. In this film, salvation must be found in following one's true destiny, from which there is no satisfactory escape.

Or consider the all-time great blockbuster and Oscar winner *Titanic* (1997). Virtually everything in the film sends the same message: do not live according to society's boring rules but by the most romantic and ideological means possible. This is not merely a happy-go-lucky attitude. Rose is saved not once but three times by her lover, Jack. The first time is when they meet and he talks her out of committing suicide; the second is when he brings her safely through the sinking of the ship. But neither of these saving acts reveals the message of the movie. The real challenge Rose deals with throughout the film is upper-class expectations. Jack teaches Rose how to escape societal rules and expectations, thereby allowing her to "live life to the fullest." In *Titanic*, this realization is salvation itself. The fact that *Titanic* won eleven Oscars and remained the highest grossing film of all time over a decade after its release suggests that the movie's "salvation message" resonated deeply with many people.

Whether it is turning from a life of crime, finding true love, realizing one's potential, gaining a skill, or outsmarting one's adversaries, the idea that "the key to life is found within" should give Christians pause. The gospel message is clear that we can do nothing to save ourselves and that our only hope of salvation is found in the sacrifice of Jesus Christ. Maslow was correct in a sense—true self-actualization is more significant than physical needs, safety, or self-esteem. But I would disagree with him about what that means. After seeking satisfaction in every place imaginable, the wisest man on earth discovered that to "fear God and keep his commandments" is the whole duty of man. In other words, we are created for God and will only find our true "self-realization" in Him.[56]

THE TRUE GOSPEL: *Testify, Clarify, and Justify*

The true gospel states that mankind was created by an all-good and all-powerful God so that we could worship, love, and serve Him. The situation got messed up when mankind disobeyed God and became His enemy. God then made a way for reconciliation by sending His only Son to die in our place. If we choose to trust in Jesus for salvation, we will be spared from God's wrath and spend forever enjoying Him in heaven. If we choose to continue in disbelief and rebellion, we will suffer forever in hell.

While evangelistic methods may vary from tract placement, to handing out Bibles, to street preaching, to long-term relationship building, true evangelism cannot be separated from this true gospel. In fact, both "evangelize" and "gospel" are translated from the same Greek root word. Evangelism is essentially "gospelling"!

The trouble is, so many people—including some Christians—have a skewed understanding of the gospel. Consider this humorous "hymn" from Monty Python's *The Meaning of Life*:

PRIEST: | *"Oh Lord, please don't burn us.*
Don't grill or toast your flock.
Don't put us on the barbecue or simmer us in stock.
Don't braise or bake or boil us or stir-fry us in a wok.
Oh please don't lightly poach us or baste us with hot fat.
Don't fricassee or roast us or boil us in a vat.
And please don't stick thy servants Lord, in a Rotissomat."

(Monty Python: The Meaning of Life)

While this is certainly irreverent, it is also an accurate reflection of the attitude many non-believers have of the Christian God. When sharing the Good News of Christ with non-believers, we have a number of misunderstandings to overcome. In order to make true disciples, then, we must first *testify* to the true gospel message. Then we should *clarify* any misconceptions or explain anything that our hearer finds confusing. Finally, we must be prepared to *justify* our belief in the truth of the gospel. Fortunately, as we will see at the end of this chapter, movies provide an excellent way to start the kinds of conversations in which these things may take place.

Testify

The apostle Paul writes in Romans 1:16 that the gospel is God's power to save anyone who believes it. Here we need to make clear exactly what someone is being saved from. In the next verses he clearly lays out mankind's problem: we naturally suppress the truth in our unrighteousness, putting us under God's wrath (Romans 1:18). So the gospel is God's power to turn His wrath away from those who believe its message.

Now that we know what the gospel saves believers *from*, we address *how* the gospel saves. Again, Paul tells us clearly: we are saved by grace, through faith—not by working for it, but by receiving it as a gift from God; and we are saved to do good works (Ephesians 2:8-10). Oddly, I have found one of the most succinct and accurate summaries of the true gospel in a Hollywood film:

JUDGE: | *"You are guilty . . . and you are free to go."*
(The Exorcism of Emily Rose)

Once we know what the gospel saves believers *from* and *how* the gospel saves, we need to understand what it is we are to have faith *in* to receive this salvation. Paul gives us a fantastic point-by-point summary of, and model for, communicating the true gospel in 1 Corinthians 15:1-7 (NET):

> *Now I want to make clear for you, brothers and sisters, the gospel that I preached to you, that you received and on which you stand, and by which you are being saved. . . . For I passed on to you as of first importance what I also received—that [1] Christ died for our sins according to the scriptures, and that [2] he was buried, and that [3] he was raised on the third day according to the scriptures, . . . and that [4] he appeared to James, then to all the apostles.*

Clarify

It may be necessary to clarify the four points Paul articulates. First, when we say "Christ," we mean Jesus Christ the God-Man; the Christ who saves is God Himself (John 1:1; Romans 10:9-13; Colossians 1:13-23; etc.). Simply saying, "Yeah, sure, I believe in Jesus," is not what Paul means. Second, we mean that Jesus died a physical death and was buried. Then, after three days, His physical body was raised from the dead. That is, His resurrection wasn't simply spiritual; it was an actual, historical fact. This is evidenced by Paul's fourth point that Jesus appeared to credible eyewitnesses after His resurrection.

Justify

Once we have stated and explained the gospel, we should also be prepared to defend it. This is called *apologetics*, which literally means "giving an answer" (1 Peter 3:15). The only way to do this effectively is to study the reasons why we believe what we believe. This will prepare us to "demolish arguments and every pretension that sets itself up against the knowledge of God," and to take "captive every thought to make it obedient to Christ" (2 Corinthians 10:5). Apologetics was central to Paul's mission (Philippians 1:7, 16), and he even made the practice a requirement for church leadership (Titus 1:9). Jude, an apostle of Jesus, echoes the same emphasis: "Although I was very eager to write to you about the salvation we share, I felt I had to write and urge you to contend for the faith that was once for all entrusted to the saints" (Jude 3).

Jesus Himself stated that people should believe in Him because of the evidence He provided for what He taught (more on that in chapter 10).[57] Although our faith is in an invisible God, our God has revealed Himself in history.[58] God wants us to take a step of faith in the light of evidence, not a leap into the dark.

Now, none of this is to say that bare apologetics, free from the influence of the Holy Spirit, can bring someone to saving faith. This creates a false dilemma in the minds of many of "the Spirit vs. logic." We must not overlook the fact that the Holy Spirit's guidance is necessary for someone to embrace sincere belief. Yet, the Spirit can use whatever means He wishes to accomplish this.

With some people He uses trials, with others an emotional experience, and others He reaches through reason. All we are expected to do is be prepared to give an account of the hope we have in Christ.

Coffee Shop Talk:

BATMAN BEGINS EVANGELISM

"So how did it go with Nita?" Renee asked Mike, after their first sips of coffee had begun to warm them.

Mike looked shocked.

"Mike, I work here—I see all! I was watching you guys from behind the counter last week, and now I'm dying to know what you were talking about."

Renee was a part-time barista at the café. She and Mike had met in a comparative religions class their freshman year. He had eventually worked up the courage to probe a bit about her spiritual life and was politely turned away from the subject. So he had simply kept up a friendly dialogue with her at the café, always hoping for a way to bring up spiritual things but being too scared of a confrontation. Now Renee was taking her break with him and pumping him for details of his personal life. Why weren't non-Christians ever afraid of probing?

"Well, if you must know, 'it' went fine. We were just hanging out anyway—it wasn't anything serious," Mike said, trying to sound casual. "We're just friends."

"For now . . ." Renee smirked.

"Yeah, well, I got into hot water at first when I brought up movies," Mike replied.

"How could movies get you in trouble?" Renee asked. "Everyone likes movies."

"I know!" Mike said a bit too loudly. "I think we just had some differences of opinion over what constitutes a good movie. It kind of turned into a debate."

"And I thought you Christians agreed on everything," Renee teased. "Maybe you just need to work on your pickup lines."

Mike laughed. "All I said was, 'Seen any good movies lately?'"

"Yes," Renee answered at once. "Okay, sorry to switch gears on you, but I actually did see a great movie last weekend—*Batman Begins*. The story line was much better than the other Batman movies, and Christian Bale is the best Batman yet."

"What did you like about the story?"

"I liked that the hero and the villain were believable, and the story was more sophisticated than some of the others," Renee answered.

Mike was impressed. Warming to the discussion, he said, "Yes, exactly. The hero started off as a vengeful vigilante and ended up fighting for true justice. The villain seemed like a good guy at first, so it was even more interesting when he turned out to be evil."

"Well, I wouldn't call him *evil*," Renee answered. "He wanted justice, too. He just tried to achieve it the wrong way."

"So you don't think that poisoning an entire city is evil?" Mike asked, surprised at this unexpected turn.

"Well, I think that we have to look at why people do things, not just what they do, before we call them evil," Renee said. "Otherwise we're just being judgmental."

"So it would be okay to kill a million people if someone had good motives?" Mike countered.

"Sure," she said, shocking him. "What about war? If we have to kill people to stop evil, then that isn't an evil thing. Haven't you taken Ethics 101 yet?" She smiled, assuming that Mike was probably going to agree with her on this one.

"Okay." Mike paused as he struggled with his response. "I

agree that war is sometimes necessary to fight evil, so we can't just say that killing is evil. But aren't some actions always evil? Like torturing babies for fun?"

"So you *have* taken Ethics 101?" Renee laughed.

"So we agree that some actions are simply evil," Mike continued. "If someone does one of those things, it isn't judgmental to say they are evil, is it?" Renee shook her head. "So the only question is . . ." Mike trailed off.

"Who decides what is evil?" Renee answered. "And that's a big problem, because everyone decides morality for themselves. Or it's cultural."

"Which culture allows torturing babies for fun?" Mike asked. "If there was such a culture, wouldn't it be right to say that it was evil?"

"Well, yeah," Renee answered, "but I don't think anyone would ever do that."

"Are you sure?" Mike asked. "The Nazis thought it was okay to torture people, and other countries judged them as being evil."

"What does this have to do with *Batman*?" Renee asked, steering the conversation back to the movie.

"A lot," Mike answered. "Why did you think the villain was more believable?"

"Because he wasn't just some lunatic—he was rational," she answered. "He had reasons for what he did."

"Were they good reasons?" Mike asked.

"Well, sort of," Renee said thoughtfully. "He wanted to rid the world of evil. The problem was that he would have killed a lot of good people, too."

"He didn't think he was killing any good people," Mike pointed out.

"But there were good people—everyday people like you and me," Renee replied. "We certainly don't deserve to be killed for anything we've done—unless you have some deep, dark past I don't know about."

"But," Mike continued, "if we can't judge people by their actions, or if morals are all cultural, then why couldn't he be right that there were no good people in the city?"

"Because," Renee thought for a moment, "he can't just impose his morality on everyone else."

"But aren't we imposing our morality on him when we say he is wrong about who is good and who is evil?" Mike asked. "If we cannot say who is right or wrong, then all morality becomes rather pointless."

Renee thought about this for a moment. "I guess in extreme cases like this we can."

"But who decides what is extreme?" Mike asked. "Doesn't this just push the problem back a step? If we keep referring to what people think about morals, we can always find exceptions."

"Yes, but I doubt that the majority of people would disagree," Renee answered.

"But what if they did? Does a majority have the ability to change what is really evil?" Mike asked. "It seems that if Hitler had won the war, then the entire Western world might have eventually agreed that killing off Jews was a good thing."

"Well, something inside us seems to tell us what is right and wrong; otherwise we wouldn't agree on anything," Renee answered. "Maybe it's because of evolution."

"Could we evolve into thinking that torture and genocide are good things?" Mike asked. "Is morality just the effect of some gene passed on by our ancestors? If so, why don't we follow it? It seems to me the fact that we often don't do what we feel is right indicates that morality is something outside of us. If it isn't, then we have no objective basis for ethics—it's all just what people feel at certain times. But how can we be obligated to follow a morality that we make up?"

"Gee, I guess that leaves God, of course," Renee replied sarcastically. "Is that where you are going with this? We need God to give us morals?"

"I wasn't going anywhere," Mike answered, smiling, "but since you brought it up—God would have the right to make the call, because He is the standard for goodness. Wouldn't that solve the problem?"

"What if I don't believe in God?" Renee asked.

"I have several good arguments that He exists if you're interested," Mike offered with a smile.

"I'm sure you do, *church boy*," Renee said with a gleam in her eye. "But it's not God's existence I have a problem with," she continued, growing more serious. "No offense, but it's your God specifically."

This was unexpected. Mike knew Renee was not a Christian, but he thought she just needed some more time to see that Christians could be cool people, too. Apparently not. His adrenaline was starting to flow, and this often indicated that he was about to say something stupid, so he tried to calm down and just let Renee explain. "What problem is that, Renee?" he asked.

She sighed. "I was hoping to avoid this because you seem like a nice guy, Mike, but the Christian God seems like a real jerk. Your God loves me so much 'that He sent His only Son to die for me' but I will burn forever in hell if I don't love Him back. How is that not crazy?"

Mike understood her thinking. "Renee," he began, "threatening someone into loving God never sounded right to me either. But that's not what the Bible actually says."

"Well," she retorted, "someone needs to tell your buddies at church then. Every time someone has tried to preach to me, it's either been 'God loves you,' or 'You're going to hell.' So which is it?"

"Let me explain how I understand the situation," Mike said, "and see if it makes more sense to you." He gulped down a large swallow of coffee in preparation.

"Both statements are true," Mike said earnestly. "God does love you, and yet you might go to hell anyway. When people focus solely on one truth or the other, the gospel might not seem to make sense. The Bible says that people are not simply unfriendly or unloving toward God, but that by choosing to rebel against God's will and refusing to worship Him, we make ourselves His enemies. Hell is punishment for *that*, not for refusing to be His 'buddy.' But because God is also merciful, He does not desire people to go to hell. So He offers us salvation through Jesus Christ. Jesus died so that we could be saved from our rebellion. Friendship with God is a benefit of salvation, not the reason for it."

"If He loves us so much, why couldn't He just forgive us?" Renee asked.

"Well, God is loving, merciful, and forgiving, but He is also good, righteous, and just. Loving someone does not mean that you excuse their evil or that you prevent them from suffering the consequences of their actions. In *Batman Begins*, Batman loved Ducard, his mentor. He even saved his life when he could have let him die. That is mercy. But when Ducard committed a heinous crime, showing how evil he truly was, Batman had no problem letting him die. That is justice."

"But if God was just, then He wouldn't let His Son die for us. He would make us pay for our sins and we'd all end up in hell," Renee objected.

"Jesus freely chose to pay our debt, preserving both God's justice and His mercy, for Jesus is God himself," Mike answered.

"The just died for the unjust. According to the apostle Paul, Jesus died for our sins, was buried, rose from the grave, and appeared to many people as proof. If we put our trust in His actions on our behalf, we will be raised from death, too, and spend forever with God in heaven. If we choose to remain God's enemies . . . well . . . then He honors that choice as well."

"This is a lot different than what I have heard before," Renee told Mike. "And it's a nice story, don't get me wrong, but lots of religions have nice stories. How can I know which one is true?" Renee asked.

"Well, the story I just told you has proof built in. That story is called the 'good news,' and it is found in the earliest of Christian beliefs. It was the eyewitness testimony of Jesus' resurrection that provided the foundation for the church. Many of these witnesses died horrifying deaths because they could not deny what they had seen. It wasn't just a nice story to them. Even today when it is a lot easier to dream up alternative explanations, the majority of Bible scholars— Christian and non-Christian—agree that at the very least Jesus died, that His tomb was found empty, and that both Jesus' disciples and His former enemies claimed to have seen Him risen from the dead. It is very difficult to explain these historical facts away."

Renee had started to fidget and look around, so Mike finished up quickly. "Renee, God gave all the light that people need to see, but He also left enough darkness for those who don't want to see. I hope you will consider where the evidence points before it's too late."

"I see," Renee replied. "Well, my break is over. You've given me a lot to think about. Thanks. I have a better understanding of what you believe and why you believe it. I guess you Christians are not all loonies after all," Renee said, smiling. "Now I've got some sleepy people to wake up."

"Okay," Mike said. "Can we talk about movies again sometime?"

"Sure," said Renee, rising from her chair.

"Great," Mike beamed. "Maybe next time we can talk about *The Chronicles of Narnia*, or *The Lord of the Rings*, or *The Passion of the* . . ."

"Nice try, pal," Renee said wryly, looking over her shoulder as she moved toward the counter. "How about one with a theme that doesn't scream *'Christianity Is True!'*"

"Name a good movie that doesn't talk about redemption, love, justice, or mercy," Mike said, "and you're on!"

CONCLUSION

As this dialogue illustrates, any movie worth watching will include some features of a true worldview. One strong feature of *Batman Begins* is morality. The film's main theme is that vigilante justice is not true justice. Some form of objective morality is being assumed here. This is an excellent starting point from which to discuss Christianity. Any time a story requires some component of the Christian worldview to make sense, you have a great opportunity to argue that Christianity must be true.

Notice in the dialogue that Mike allowed the conversation to flow naturally. He moved from an implied moral argument for God to asking more questions. He did not launch into the rational arguments for God, even though Renee professed unbelief. He wisely kept asking questions until he reached the real issue, at which point he *testified* to the truth of the gospel. He discovered that Renee did not have an intellectual issue with the existence of a supreme being. Rather, she had a problem with the gospel as she understood it. In response, Mike *clarified* Renee's misunderstanding of the gospel. This saved a lot of time and avoided possible rabbit trails that might have kept them distracted from the true gospel message.

Also, when the time came to present the gospel, Mike did not water it down or use manipulative emotional appeals. He gave it to her straight.

Further, he included in his discussion of the gospel message the reasons why it can be trusted. That is, he *justified* the gospel. After a good discussion about objective standards, it was not time for testimony sharing. Rather, at this point, Mike needed to show Renee that her reasons for disbelief were unsound in light of the true message of the gospel and the strong historical evidence for the resurrection of Jesus.

Finally, Mike did not push for "a decision." Instead, he simply let Renee know that the situation was urgent ("before it's too late") before she returned to work. This allowed him to end on a friendly, confident note without backing down from the truth. This should keep the door open for future conversations. Mike successfully delivered the message and backed it up. The rest is in God's hands.

REFLECTION QUESTIONS

1. What can the gospel do, according to Romans 1:16?

2. What are the four elements of the gospel message according to 1 Corinthians 15:1-5?

3. How are Christians to fight in defense of the gospel according to 2 Corinthians 10:3-5?

DISCUSSING MOVIES PHILOSOPHICALLY:
Is Reality Virtual or Veritable?

WHAT DO WE KNOW?

MORPHEUS: | *"I'm trying to free your mind ... but I can only show you the door. You're the one that has to walk through it."*
(The Matrix)

In the previous chapter, we considered how our culture's hesitancy to acknowledge human sinfulness can be a hindrance to evangelism. In this chapter, we'll discuss a second potential obstacle to evangelism in the twenty-first century—the postmodern skepticism about the nature of reality. Fortunately, just as movies can provide excellent opportunities to discuss the gospel message of salvation, they can also open doors to conversations about philosophical issues that might be a hindrance to faith.

If this is beginning to sound a bit cerebral, perhaps an illustration will help. I remember the first time I met someone who questioned the objective nature of reality and truth. I was with my college group leader sharing the gospel on campus. After we presented the gospel to one particular student, he replied, "It's great that you believe in Christianity, but it isn't true for me." This response threw me for a loop. I was prepared to respond to people who objected that Christianity wasn't true, but I was not ready for someone to tell me that it might be true—*but only for me.* As it turned out, this was my introduction to postmodernism.

Before we continue, it's important that we define a couple of terms. The first is "modernism." Modernism refers to the belief that all truth can be determined through science or reason. The primary means of discovering the truth in modernism is through observation and experimentation. Post-modernism, by contrast, doubts our powers of observation and, as a result, calls objective reality into question. For instance, we can all think of times when we have been fooled by our senses—through hallucinations, mirages, dreams, or optical illusions. Thus, postmodern thinkers began asking question such as, *How do we know our senses aren't fooling us?* or *How do we know that the pictures in our mind represent what reality is actually like?* Unfortunately, the methods of modernism (science experiments and logical arguments) could not answer these questions, because science and reason both assume that we perceive reality as it is.

As you can see, postmodernism describes a change not only in *what* people think but also in *how* they think. Postmodernism argues that all we can know for certain are the ideas that dwell in our own minds. That means my ideas are just as good as anyone else's—even if they disagree with me. This leads to the conclusion that we all have equal say in what is real—things may be "true for you" but not necessarily "true for me."

This shift in thought patterns has important implications for both the presentation and defense of Christianity. The kind of apologetics that relies on common sense and logical argumentation has become more difficult to sustain. Prior to the late 1980s, for instance, the best source of information for the budding apologist was something like Josh McDowell's *Evidence That Demands a Verdict*, which was essentially a list of facts supporting the key assertions of Christianity. But postmoderns would argue that these facts are not self-interpreting. That is, there may be more than one possible (if not plausible) explanation for any given fact. This has made it more important than ever to be able to establish a basic starting point that does not rely on questionable presuppositions.

In this chapter, we will demonstrate that truth is objective (based on reality, not our thoughts about reality), absolute (true for everyone), and knowable. This will not be as difficult as you might imagine, because the postmodern has not truly given up on objective reality. She may say she has, but watch her cross the street (postmoderns still look both ways) or access bank accounts (postmoderns still apply absolute truth to their bank statement), and you will see that in virtually every area of life—except religion and morality—postmoderns are every bit as modern as their predecessors.

To conclude, we will see how popular movies can provide us with opportunity to discuss this important truth.

KNOWING THAT WE KNOW

BITSEY: | *"There is no truth, only perspectives."*

ZACK: | *"Can't say that. If you say there's no truth, you're claiming it's true there's no truth. It's a logical contradiction."*

BITSEY: | *"Working on our philosophy merit badge are we, Zack?"*

ZACK: | *"It's just my perspective."*   (The Life of David Gale)

There is an old fable about several blind men who happen upon an elephant in the jungle. One touches the trunk and thinks he has found a snake. The next man feels the leg and believes it to be a tree. The third man feels the elephant's side and says it's a wall. Another man touches its tusk and thinks it's a spear. Yet another touches its ear and believes it's a fan. The point of the story is that although people claim to know the truth, because we are all limited in our perspective, we can only grasp limited aspects of it.

There is an element of truth in this story, but it is ultimately and terminally flawed in its message. Can you see the problem? What makes the story work is that the men were all wrong, and we, the audience of the story, *know* they were wrong. The trouble is you cannot know something is wrong unless you know what is right; the story would mean nothing if we were unaware that the men had found an elephant. Ironically, this story is often told in order to correct people who claim to be right and call opposing views false. Yet the person telling the story knows the truth about the elephant and that all the blind men are wrong! In other words, the intended message is self-defeating. In trying to prove that truth is relative and reality is unknowable, the story instead proves that truth is in fact absolute and reality is knowable.

Truth is a statement that matches reality. So if reality exists, truth must exist. That's plain enough. But if we argue that reality does not exist, we are still making a truth claim that presumably matches reality. This basic flaw infects every argument against truth and reality.

Throughout the 1990s and early 2000s several movies explored the notion that we might not really know reality. Films like *Total Recall* (1990), *The Matrix* (1999), *The Thirteenth Floor* (1999), and *Vanilla Sky* (2001) all relied on some alternative reality for their stories to work. What they all do, however, is show that someone actually knows reality—the audience! Like the elephant fable above, these stories would not be interesting if the viewers were not convinced of *real* reality.

What all this means is that while we can certainly be mistaken at times about what is real, there is indeed a reality to know. Mistakes actually prove the point. We would not know there were such things as hallucinations or illusions if we did not have reality with which to compare them. Most alleged disproof of objective reality is simply an issue of judgment or interpretation of data, not our direct knowledge of the world. So the real issue is what is true—not whether or not there is such thing as truth.

RELATIVE VS. ABSOLUTE TRUTHS

WINSTON SMITH: | *"There is truth, and there is untruth."*   (1984)

Similar confusion occurs around the issue of relative statements. Some statements are only true in certain contexts. The statement "Giraffes are tall," for instance, depends upon what I am comparing to the height of giraffes.

If the statement is comparing giraffes to other animals, then it is true. If it is comparing them to skyscrapers, then it would be false. However, once we know the context the statement is assuming, the truth or falsity of the statement is easy to determine. The point is this: Relative *terms* do not make for relative *truths*. All truth values are absolute in their own context, because all statements either correspond to reality or they do not.

OBJECTIVE VS. SUBJECTIVE TRUTHS

When we say something is "objectively true," we usually mean that it is true regardless of what anyone thinks about it. We are speaking of something that either corresponds to reality (is true), or doesn't correspond to reality (is false). For example, if I say that ice cream melts at temperatures above thirty-two degrees Fahrenheit, I am not simply telling you what I think. I'm offering an objective statement about ice cream. However, if I say that ice cream tastes delicious, I am telling you something about me and my experience of eating it. Thus, "ice cream tastes delicious" is a subjective statement. But it is not a subjective truth. If the statement about ice cream's taste to me is true, it is true regardless of what anyone else thinks about ice cream. The statement "ice cream is delicious to me" cannot be made false by someone who disagrees, even though taste itself is subjective. So, we can speak of subjective *statements*, but not subjective *truths*. All statements either correspond to reality or they don't.

TRUTH AND CONSEQUENCES

The price to pay for truth is the possibility of falsehood. We can certainly be grateful that we can perceive the world as it is and know the truth. However, if a statement is true, then anything that contradicts it is false. This means that our telling the truth may cause offense at times in this culture that wishes to affirm everything.

Some people try to avoid offending others with the truth by appealing to Matthew 7:1 (NASB): "Do not judge so that you will not be judged." This strategy is employed by believers and unbelievers alike. And there's good reason for this. In a society in which tolerance is a preeminent value, "judging" another person's ideas or lifestyle is a significant offense. Nevertheless, this is clearly not what Jesus meant when He taught us not to judge one another. The next verse in Matthew confirms that Jesus is concerned with the reasons for which we judge: "For in the way you judge, you will be judged; and by your standard of measure, it will be measured to you." In the context of the passage, Jesus means that we are guilty of sinful judgment if we judge others self-righteously. So, while we must not judge according to our own fallen standards, simply stating facts is not judgment.[59]

In fact, Scripture actually commands us to judge. Jesus taught that we should judge, not according to appearance, but with "right judgment" (John 7:24). Wisdom involves judging situations (Proverbs 1:2); testing the spirits requires judging messages (1 John 4:1); confronting sinning believers necessitates judging actions (Matthew 18:15; 1 Corinthians 5:3-13; 6:2-4); correcting those in opposition demands judging doctrine (2 Timothy 2:25).

Any time we differentiate between one thing and another, we have judged. How could we even tell the difference between right and wrong without judging? So the next time someone accuses you of being judgmental, do this: Ask yourself if the statement you made was a statement of fact or just your own ideas. If it is just your opinion, apologize and restate what you said. If not, simply ask them, "Is it your judgment that I am wrong for judging?" This isn't being clever; it's being consistent.

As with the previous coffeehouse dialogues, the one that follows puts the content of this chapter into practice. However, it may be helpful before we proceed to offer a brief synopsis of the movie being discussed.

The plot of *The Matrix* (1999) assumes that machines have taken over the planet and have created an imaginary world that is streamed electronically into the minds of human subjects, who believe this world is real. Meanwhile, the humans' physical bodies are trapped in cocoons, where they serve as "living batteries" to power the machines. The protagonist, Neo, escapes the Matrix with the help of a few other rebels so that he is free to experience the "real world." Or is he?

Coffee Shop Talk:

MATRIX EVANGELISM

Renee called Mike on Thursday to invite him to an informal discussion group at the coffeehouse that she sat in on when she wasn't busy with customers. The group was led by a popular philosophy professor. She had overheard that this week they would be discussing *The Matrix* trilogy. Mike immediately agreed since it was one of his favorite film series.

When he arrived, he found several students whom he had seen around campus warming up with favorite quotes from the films. He greeted a few of them and met Dr. Matthews, the professor who led the discussions. Then he got a drink and sat down to see how it would go.

Dr. Matthews motioned that they were going to begin. "Tonight," he began, "I would like to discuss one of the most talked-about films of recent years—*The Matrix*." He continued, "So here is the question: Did the film give an adequate answer to the question of what the Matrix is?"

One student spoke up and said, "Yeah, the Matrix was the machine world's way of controlling humans. It was a program like virtual reality."

"Okay, good," began Dr. Matthews. "And what is the 'machine world'?"

"The real world," ventured another student. "Morpheus explained that to Neo after he first came out of the Matrix: 'Welcome to the *real* world.'"

Nods followed as the students remembered the dramatic moment when Neo opened his eyes for the first time to see the real Morpheus standing over him.

"And how does this relate to our own world?" asked Dr. Matthews.

"It doesn't," answered the first student. "We're not in the Matrix—this *is* the real world." He picked up a spoon and tapped it against his mug. "There *is* a spoon!" he proclaimed, eliciting laughter from the group.

"Is there?" Dr. Matthews asked. "How can you prove that the world you see around you is the real world? How can you be sure that your thoughts of the spoon correspond to a real spoon that exists outside your mind?"

The student tapped the spoon again as if to say, *Can you not hear that?*

Dr. Matthews was ready. "How can you be sure that your thoughts of the spoon hitting the mug correspond to a real spoon hitting a mug that exists outside your mind?"

This caused a pause. No one could come up with a test that did not depend on his thoughts being accurate in the first place. Mike felt a bit out of his league, but he needed to say something. *After all,* he thought, *if we can't trust our senses and thoughts, then nothing is definite.* Worse, he noticed Renee watching him. If he could not defend the knowability of reality, then everything else they had talked about was useless. He decided to give it a shot. He tried to turn the question around. "Dr. Matthews," he asked, "is there any reason to think we *don't* know reality?"

This led to some raised eyebrows around the circle, but Dr. Matthews didn't hesitate. "Certainly," he responded, glad to have someone thinking seriously about the subject. "For example, we've all thought we saw something that wasn't real—mirages, hallucinations, optical illusions, and so on. These are evidence that our senses cannot be trusted to deliver accurate information about the external sensible world."

"I see," answered Mike. "But don't these occurrences actually prove the opposite?"

Everyone turned to Mike with confused expressions, and Dr. Matthews smiled. "Continue," he said.

"Well," Mike began, "those are all examples of things that we know do not match reality. Mirages and optical illusions are mistakes in judging what our senses report—like thinking that a stick bends in water when really the light makes it appear bent. Hallucinations are sensory mistakes, yes, but we only recognize them as mistakes because we can compare them to reality."

"But those examples do show that what we think we know is not always the case," Dr. Matthews began. "For example, you probably think the chair you are sitting on is solid—and it certainly appears to be so. But we know that in reality—if you will—it is made up of atoms. The appearance is not the reality in this case."

Mike hoped he was not digging his own philosophical grave, but he plunged on. "Do you think this is an error in perception or an error in our judgment of those perceptions? Maybe the problem is simply imprecise language. Saying the chair is solid when it is actually made up of atoms does not change the fact that my hand does not go through a chair like it goes through water. If that's all I mean by 'solid,' then the belief is not false. And once again, aren't we relying on sense data to reveal that the chair is made of atoms? It seems to me that if we say 'here is an example of our senses fooling us,' then we are trusting in what our senses are telling us to conclude that we can't trust what our senses are telling us!"

The other students were beginning to enjoy this. Mike's arguments did seem to make sense.

Dr. Matthews offered his response. "You are right that to some extent it is my senses that tell me not to trust my senses. But it is really the combination of my senses plus my reason that suggests to me that my usual observations only indicate what the world seems like to me and do not reveal what the world is *really* like."

This was going well beyond Mike's knowledge base. He did not really follow all the details of Dr. Matthews's argument, but his main question still seemed relevant.

"I hope I'm not just being dim," Mike began, "but it still seems to me that you are making what you think are accurate descriptions of the world as it really is. If it is true that we don't know the real world, then isn't that a statement about the real world that you know?"

"Yes," answered Dr. Matthews. "But let's return to the example of your chair. You admit it is not as it appears to be. Your senses tell you that there is a solid object before you, yet reason tells you that it is made up of atoms. If you were the size of an atom, you would think a chair was millions of large objects floating around in space. So which of those perceptions is accurate?"

"I think they're both accurate," Mike said. "I might see a grape as being very large if I were an ant, or I might perceive raindrops as giant deadly blobs . . ."

"Like in *A Bug's Life*!" someone interrupted.

"Another excellent movie!" Mike replied. "But isn't that what they actually are? Neither perception is inaccurate. Perspective might affect my language or relationship to a thing, but I'm describing the same thing in any case. Different perspectives of an object surely do not make that object unreal, do they? I don't see how the fact that things appear different from different angles or perspectives threatens our knowledge of reality. Our reason allows us to go beyond sensory appearance, as you pointed out; but that just tells me that our reason helps us to know reality. I don't know that it helps to say our senses plus reason tell us that our senses plus reason are false."

This was getting heavy. Another round of coffee was ordered before the discussion continued. Dr. Matthews responded to Mike's last question with a rather uncomfortable conclusion: "It is true that bringing in reason does not solve the issue, but I've never felt that there was really a problem. I would return to the internal/external distinction. My internal reality—which I can know—is that I don't know external reality—and may never know it."

They both stared at one another for a minute. Mike finally asked, "You don't think it is a problem to say we don't know reality?" The students all turned to Dr. Matthews.

"No," he replied, "not in any practical sense. We can still lead coherent, moral lives without knowing the world beyond our senses and thoughts."

"I'm not sure how ethics can work without reality," Mike said. "I wonder how you justify things like the value of humanity or other basic moral principles without a knowable reality. For example, if I don't really know that the object in front of me is a person, how can I decide whether or not it would be okay to kill it?"

"If all of us perceive reality the same way, then it is not a problem," answered Dr. Matthews.

"And how could we know that?" asked Mike. "This was one of the things that really bothered me about the *Matrix* films. You asked in the beginning of the discussion if the film gave an adequate answer to the question of what the Matrix was. I'm not convinced it did. What Morpheus and the other escapees perceived as being the Machine World could have simply been another level of the Matrix. If skepticism about knowing reality is taken as one's starting point, there is no way out. Maybe we need to begin instead with what seems to be the case and go from there."

"All right guys," Renee interrupted, jangling her store keys. "This has been fascinating, but as the Oracle says, 'Everything that has a beginning has an end.' It's closing time!" The students groaned with disappointment.

Mike threw in some closing statements as they began rearranging the chairs. "I think maybe there is a basic problem with the idea that we only know ideas in our mind. We never speak of things as ideas unless we know them to be simply ideas. For example, we do not go to the store and ask for the idea of bread; we want *bread*. The fact that we can even make this distinction seems to indicate that we can tell the difference between a mere idea and a real object. Skepticism seems to me to be one step more complicated than it needs to be, and it's a theory that can't be disproved, even if we did wake up in a pod!

"But if we begin with the view that we do know reality, we have a chance of explaining what most people take for granted. Maybe this is simplistic, but I can't see any good reason to reject it!"[60]

CONCLUSION

As you can see, even science fiction movies can do a lot of damage to one's worldview if they are not considered critically. If you had trouble following the conversation, don't despair. I wanted you to see that even a sophisticated philosopher can be approached with good, sound reasoning on your side. All Mike did in the above conversation was keep bringing the conversation back to the problems of skepticism. In short, the point is this: it is up to the Christian apologist to show that if knowability is required to prove non-knowability, then non-knowability is absurd.

Although we may be wrong about what the truth is, we must agree that it does exist. Even if some have a difficult time discerning how we know truth, we do know that it can be known. What this means is that while we can and should argue about what is true, we should never call either truth itself or our ability to apprehend it into question.[61]

REFLECTION QUESTIONS

1. What is the problem with statements like, "No one can know truth," "Truth does not exist," or "Truth is different for everybody"?

2. How might you reply to statements like, "We cannot know reality," "Hallucinations prove we cannot be sure about reality," or "We might just be brains in some mad scientist's lab"?

3. If the experience of reality cannot convince someone that we know reality, could any argument ever do so?

DISCUSSING MOVIES THEOLOGICALLY:
Is God a Delusion or Deity?

CAN GOD'S EXISTENCE BE PROVED?

ELLIE:	*"All right. So what's more likely ... that an all-powerful, mysterious God created the universe and then decided not to give any proof of His existence or that He simply doesn't exist at all and that we've created Him so we didn't have to feel so small and alone?"*
JOSS:	*"I don't know. I couldn't imagine living in a world where God didn't exist. I wouldn't want to."*
ELLIE:	*"How do you know you're not deluding yourself? I mean, for me, I'd need proof."*
JOSS:	*"Proof. Did you love your father?"*
ELLIE:	*"What?"*
JOSS:	*"Your dad, did you love him?"*
ELLIE:	*"Yes, very much."*
JOSS:	*"Prove it."* (Contact)

If the Bible is what it claims to be—the very Word of God—then there are two things that must be true: God exists and God has spoken. But if we are talking with someone who denies the very existence of God, it does little good to explain what God has done or said! Christians usually take the existence of God for granted when sharing the gospel with non-believers, but some people need to hear an argument for God's existence before they will be open to receiving the gospel.

In the movie *Contact* (1997), Joss makes a great point when he challenges Ellie to "prove" she loved her dad. Asking for absolute proof of something like love is not fair; but it is no less fair than Ellie's asking for "scientific" proof for God. During the film, I wanted Joss to offer a good argument or two for God's existence, but they might have fallen on deaf ears if Ellie had not first understood that asking for scientific proof for God is like asking for scientific proof for love.

Proof for the existence of God cannot come directly from the physical sciences. It's not that scientists aren't intelligent people. It's simply that their knowledge, like everyone else's, is limited to the areas in which they have been trained. Such issues simply lie beyond the scope of scientific inquiry, which cannot address the existence of an immaterial God. This does not mean we cannot use scientific facts as evidence to support theological conclusions; it simply means that science has no ultimate authority in matters that are properly investigated by theology.

CHANTILAS:	*"I realized science couldn't answer any of the really interesting questions. So I turned to philosophy. Been searching for God ever since. Who knows, I may pick up a rock and it'll say underneath 'Made by God.' The universe is full of surprises."*
GALLAGHER:	*"That would be a big one."* (Red Planet)

Fortunately for us, the Bible teaches that there is evidence available for all people—scientists and non-scientists alike—pointing to God's existence. Paul tells us in Romans 1 and 2 that creation itself testifies to God's existence. Beginning with this assumption, people have used the created order in several ways to argue for the existence of God. In this chapter, we will look at a few of the most popular. The first two will argue from the existence of the universe and its design, and the second two will focus on human instincts regarding morality and desire.

Bear in mind as you read that there is no "silver bullet" argument appropriate to all situations or objections. These four arguments will appeal to different people for different reasons. Sometimes someone will need to hear all four. Because human beings have minds, hearts, and wills, we should seek to satisfy the whole person in our presentation. The mind may be most satisfied by the creator and design arguments. The argument from desire touches the emotional level, because it seeks to explain a universal human feeling. A person's will may be moved more by the moral argument, which shows not only that an ultimate lawgiver exists, but that we must bow to Him as His creatures. These arguments are not intended to force someone to believe in God. Neither are they absolute proofs, such that no reasonable person could possibly deny them. But they do help people understand that for Christians, faith is not blind.

FROM CREATION TO THE CREATOR

Consider the old question about the chicken and the egg—you know, which came first? The problem, of course, is that if every chicken came from an egg and every egg came from a chicken, then we could never reach an answer. But this problem hints at a solution. Just how far back can the chicken-egg-chicken chain go? It cannot go on forever. It has to stop somewhere. Moreover, the procession must begin with something that is not from a previous chicken or egg. Otherwise, the series would never end. The same goes for all other chains in the universe—trees and seeds, parents and children, even the formation of galaxies. If we apply this idea to the whole universe, it appears we need an explanation for the universe itself. If chickens come from eggs, what do universes come from? A skeptic might respond that the universe had no beginning. But this position has become more difficult to defend in recent years in light of ever-increasing scientific evidence for the Big Bang theory. This evidence includes:

- *The Second Law of Thermodynamics,* which states that the usable energy in the universe is running down. It is clear that what is running down had to begin to run down; therefore, the universe had a beginning.

- *Galactic Expansion,* a prediction verified by Edwin Hubble's discovery of the red shift in 1927, showed that the galaxies are moving away from each other and must have originated from a central point (at the beginning of the universe).

- *Cosmic Microwave Background Radiation,* the predicted radiation left over from the Big Bang, was discovered by scientists Penzias and Wilson in 1965. The temperature ripples in this background radiation, also predicted by Big Bang theorists, was discovered in 1992 by astronomer George Smoot who called them "the fingerprints of the maker."[62]

You might be wondering, What if science is wrong? Interestingly, philosophical reflection leads to the same conclusion that modern science does. No matter what is being counted, it is impossible to have an infinite number of anything. Sure, it was fun on the playground to claim that we were so strong that we could lift "infinity pounds." But in reality, this makes no sense. An "infinitieth number" is impossible, because all numbers are finite (limited). You cannot add up a bunch of limited things to reach an unlimited amount. We can use infinity as an abstract mathematical idea, but an actual infinite number of things cannot exist in reality.

Everything that has an end has a beginning. Try to imagine a one-ended stick. You can't, for the limit of the stick cannot only be on one end. If either end were unlimited, the stick would be unlimited in length. The same thing is true of the number of moments in time before now. Since we are at one end (limit) of the chain of moments, this chain had to start somewhere. And if everything in the universe is part of a limited chain, then the whole universe had a beginning. And if the universe began, it requires a beginner.[63]

Science and philosophy agree that the universe has not always existed and that things cannot create themselves. Things that have not always existed must have been created by something else. Thus if we trace the chain all the way back to the beginning, we must find something that has always existed and that explains all the things that have not always existed. The best explanation for this is the eternal God. Agnostic astronomer Robert Jastrow put it this way: "For the scientist who has lived by his faith in the power of reason, the story ends like a bad dream. He has scaled the mountains of ignorance; he is about to conquer the highest peak; as he pulls himself over the final rock, he is greeted by a band of theologians who have been sitting there for centuries."[64]

FROM DESIGN TO THE DESIGNER

ELLIE: *"Do you think there's people on other planets?"*

TED: *"I don't know ... but I guess I'd say if it is just us, it seems like an awful waste of space."*   (Contact)

Contrary to Ted and Ellie's opinion in the movie *Contact*, there is a reason for all the seemingly wasted space around the earth. Psalm 19 tells us that "the heavens declare the glory of God; the skies proclaim the work of his hands." In other words, the awe we experience when we consider the vastness of creation points to God.[65] Just as a limited creation implies an unlimited Creator, the design within creation implies a designer.

Whenever we see design, we assume from experience that it came from a designer. We can tell the difference between sand dunes and sand castles, for instance, because we see purposeful design in the castles. None of us would happen upon a sandcastle and believe that it arrived there by chance. Furthermore, when we speak of design we mean a specific, complex design—

not simply a pattern of some sort. It is the difference between "BDHIGE-HGDVNB," which is complex but has no design, "BBBBBBBB," which has design but is not complex, and "Be back at 8 p.m.," which is both designed and complex. When we see complex, specific design, we recognize it as the result of an intelligent being.

The same can be said for creation. There is much design evident in it—from the smallest life form to the largest galaxies. In the movie *Contact*, alien intelligence is discovered when the aliens communicate a short, simple, but non-random series of numbers into space. Carl Sagan, who wrote the story, believed that all it takes to assume an intelligent creator is four non-random numbers. Interestingly, the letter sequence in the genetic "alphabet" is also only four in number. Yet the amount of information produced by that code in even a single cell is greater than that found in Webster's dictionary! Sagan himself stated that the genetic information in the human brain, if written out in English, would fill some twenty million volumes. If four prime numbers in sequence require an intelligent creator, then so too do the twenty million volumes of information found in the human brain.

The universe itself shows purpose and design, as well. Astrophysicist Hugh Ross lists over one hundred finely tuned features of our universe (from the average distance between galaxies to the decay rate of the proton); of our solar system (from our galaxy size to the number of moons); and of our planet (from the number of forest fires to soil mineralization) that are all necessary for the existence of life as we know it. Ross has calculated the odds of all these necessary requirements for life arising from random chance, and they are stunning. If there were 10,000,000,000,000,000,000,000 (a sextillion) planets in the universe, there would be only a 1 in 10^{138} chance that any one of them could support life. To gain some perspective on how large the number 10^{138} is, consider that the number of atoms in the entire universe is only 10^{70}. This makes the odds of this finely tuned universe occurring by random chance essentially zero.[66]

Because design is evident at every level of the universe, we must logically infer that it was created by an intelligent designer.

FROM MORAL LAWS TO THE MORAL LAWMAKER

MURPHY:	*"Do not kill. Do not rape. Do not steal. These are principles which every man of every faith can embrace."*
CONNOR:	*"These are not polite suggestions. These are codes of behavior, and those of you that ignore them will pay the dearest cost."* (The Boondock Saints)

All people seem to know deep down that some things are right and some things are wrong. Another way to say this is that all people recognize some sort of moral law. By moral law we mean a law that describes what people *should* do, not what they *actually* do. If we based our moral codes on what people actually did, we would be in trouble! Yet even people who claim that morality is simply based on our own desires believe that some things are truly wrong. This universal knowledge of right and wrong suggests that there is a higher moral law than just our individual desires.

Some people think this moral code originates with and is limited to society or religion. But the fact that different societies can legitimately judge one another (in the way the Nazis were judged at the Nuremberg trials) is just one piece of evidence to the contrary. Neither society, nor geographical borders, nor religions overthrow humanity's basic moral awareness and obligation to do the right thing.

So where do we get these ideas? Based on our experience, we know that laws require lawgivers. If, as the Bible says, our moral awareness comes from an ultimate Lawgiver,[67] we would expect to find exactly what we observe—a moral code that is universal for all humanity.

Atheism, on the other hand, can provide no higher basis for morality. Because there is no higher authority than mankind, each person becomes his own standard of morality. All that is left is to see which person or persons become the most powerful. Hitler took this idea seriously and almost spread his evil through the entire world. Karl Marx, the father of communism, discarded religion for Darwinian evolution, and his successor Joseph Stalin caused eighteen million deaths. Another thirty million people were killed under Chairman Mao, yet another follower of atheistic communism. The twentieth century saw 188 million people killed under such regimes (up from forty million in the nineteenth century—a 470 percent increase). Clearly, these ideas have consequences.

When we try to base human morality on mankind we end up with no objective standard by which to judge between good and evil. Only in a world with objective morals can anyone really claim to be morally right or to judge another person's actions as morally wrong.[68] Where there is no lawgiver, there is only survival of the fittest.

FROM DESIRE FOR THE TRANSCENDENT TO THE TRANSCENDENT GOD

KNIGHT:	*"I want knowledge. Not belief. Not surmise. But knowledge. I want God to put out His hand towards me, show His face, speak to me."*
DEATH:	*"But He is silent."*
KNIGHT:	*"I cry to Him in the dark, but there seems to be no one there."*
DEATH:	*"Perhaps there is no one there."*
KNIGHT:	*"Then life is a senseless terror. No man can live with Death and know that everything is nothing."* (The Seventh Seal)

Human beings have a natural desire that never seems to be satisfied by the things of this world. Of course, when we feel hunger we can be satisfied with food. When we desire to breathe, we can be satisfied with oxygen. But humans also want more than what this life offers. They desire transcendence. This is true in every culture. Somewhere deep down, all people desire to know that there is "more to life than this." To put this another way, mankind is inherently religious.

We find a sense of significance in ourselves and our lives that requires this transcendence. Not only can atheism not provide an objective standard for morality, it leaves us with no hope, and no ultimate meaning for life. Nothing we do would have eternal significance if our existence simply ceased at death. It may take billions of years for all people to die, but eventually nothing anyone had ever done would matter. The best explanation for this desire is that transcendence and everlasting meaning exists. As C. S. Lewis said, "If I find in myself a desire which no experience in this world can satisfy, the most probable explanation is that I was made for another world."[69] This other world must be without end, and must reflect the values of actions taken in our previous life, if our actions are to have true significance.

Now, someone may look for transcendence in the wrong place, but at least they know to look. The testimony of atheists who have convinced themselves that there is nothing else beyond the physical world is revealing. Atheist philosopher Bertrand Russell lamented, "It is odd, isn't it? I care passionately for this world, and many things and people in it, and yet . . . what is it all? There *must* be something more important, one feels, though I don't *believe* there is."[70]

If, on the other hand, someone claims that simply getting more of this world will satisfy them, we can easily show that this is untrue. From Solomon, one of the wealthiest men of antiquity, who said, "All is vanity," to John D. Rockefeller who, when asked how much money was enough, answered, "Just a little bit more," we have the entirety of human experience to show that ultimate satisfaction in this life is impossible. It is up to Christians, then, to show that our ultimate desire can only be fulfilled by an ultimate God.[71]

Coffee Shop Talk:

CONNECTING WITH *CONTACT*

After the philosophical discussion group, Renee asked Mike if he would be interested in taking Nita out again, this time on a double date with Renee and her friend Bert.

As it turned out, one of the campus groups Bert belonged to was hosting a movie night. Renee suggested that they begin there and follow up with free coffee at the café afterward. Never one to say no to free coffee, Mike made the call. Nita agreed, and they all met in Bert's dorm.

Bert was a physics major, and he and his colleagues liked to unwind at the end of the school week with a movie. They enjoyed science fiction and other science-related films, because they enjoyed picking them apart after viewing. As Mike, Nita, and Renee entered the room, they overheard someone loudly complaining, "You can't hear explosions in space, and ships can't fly like that!" The rebuke to this critic was immediate and decisive: "*Star Wars* still rules, so shut up!"

"Guys, this is Bert," Renee announced to Mike and Nita. It was Bert who had rebuked the *Star Wars* critic.

"Good to meet you. I hear you're both Christians."

"Bert!" exclaimed Renee.

"It's okay," said Mike, looking back at Bert. "Guilty as charged!"

Bert smiled and said, "Look, you can believe whatever you want, but we're scientists here and the movie tonight is definitely in favor of rationality and knowledge. I hope you won't be offended."

Mike looked over at Nita who was wincing and answered, "Our only concern is that it is accurate in its portrayal of scientific fact." Bert smiled widely at this.

The movie was *Contact*, a film written by the late atheist astronomer Carl Sagan. It was not nearly as bad as Mike or Nita expected. There were some jabs at religion, and Christianity was not very well represented by the religious character. But in the end, the hard scientist hero became somewhat softened by her experiences beyond the lab. When the movie ended, the two couples and a few students headed over to the café where Renee got them all complimentary drinks.

"What did you think of the movie, Mike?" Bert asked when they were all seated.

"Great story," he began, "but I don't think it gave Christianity a fair shot."

Groans followed, but Bert seemed genuinely interested when he asked, "How so?"

"The Christian character was immoral," Bert began, "and too much of a fideist." He threw in this last term to sound a bit more sophisticated, something he assumed the scientists would appreciate. "A fideist," he explained, "is someone who thinks faith is irrational or unable to be proved—so people should just have faith despite any evidence."

"I thought that's just what faith was!" groused one of the science students. "I put my faith in facts!"

"Me too," replied Mike and took a long sip of his coffee. Surprised stares greeted him, so he continued. "Belief in God can be inherited from parents or taken on faith, but I think there are good arguments for God's existence that do not rely on mere hopes."

"Like what?" the first student asked.

"Well, you all agree that the universe has not always existed, right?" Mike asked. Everyone nodded. "Okay," he continued, "then what caused it to come into existence?"

"Nothing!" blurted one of the freshmen.

"So it's more scientific to think the universe came into being by nothing than by something? Where else in science are there effects without causes?" Mike responded.

"Nothing cannot cause something," Bert said. "But here's your problem: you're going to say God caused the universe. So what caused God?"

"Nothing caused God," Mike answered, and before the freshman could object he added, "God is uncaused. He simply exists."

"You can't just say 'the universe needs a cause so my God exists,'" said Bert. "Why couldn't it be two gods, or the Muslim God?"

"At this point, I'm only arguing that God exists, not which religion's god is the right one. That has to be decided on other grounds. But your issue seems to be whether or not God exists at all."

Bert nodded and said, "Fair enough. But I don't have enough faith to trust in some old man up in heaven that made everything. You'll have to do some major convincing to get me to believe. And leave religion out of it!"

"You have every right to ask for evidence," Mike answered. "Christianity does not ask for blind faith. So, besides religion, what would you suggest as a means of inquiry?"

"Well, scientific proof would be nice." This was followed by nods all around the group. Renee had perked up, and suddenly Nita joined in.

"Science can't say anything about God. Science studies only the physical world. God is not physical."

"That's right, Nita. It's not fair to ask for proof from a method that can't possibly supply it," Mike said. "Bert, remember in *Contact* when Joss asked Ellie if she loved her dad and then asked her to prove it? She couldn't—at least not in the way she demanded that Joss prove God—because love is not an object of science either. Asking science to provide proof for God is like asking biology to explain why a car won't run." There was laughter at this.

"Then what besides religion can say anything about God?" asked Bert.

"The word *science* used to just mean 'knowledge,'" Mike replied.

"Before science became so narrow as to only apply to physical things it was called *philosophy*. Philosophy is an acceptable method for investigating God, because it studies all of reality."

"Okay, so what does philosophy have to say about God?" Bert asked.

"Let's start with a premise that everyone can agree on: things exist."

"That's a pretty safe starting point!" Bert laughed. "Okay, things exist."

"Where did the things that exist today come from?" Mike asked.

"From other things," Bert responded.

Mike nodded and said, "You mean like trees come from nuts?" Bert nodded, waiting for something interesting to be said. Mike took a sip and continued. "And the nuts come from other trees, and so on and so on. Where does it stop—or I should say, where did it start?"

"At the Big Bang singularity," Bert said authoritatively. "At the Big Bang, all matter and energy exploded into being. It separated and cooled, forming galaxies and stars and planets. Science has proven this, so don't try to argue that God made it all in a week!"

"We agreed not to talk about religion, so why are you bringing God into it?" Mike asked seriously, then cracked a smile and everyone laughed. "All right, next question: What caused the Big Bang?"

"We know what happened a small fraction of a second afterward, but there are a lot of theories as to how it was caused. Is this where you're going to insert God?"

"Would that be wrong?" Mike asked.

"Yes, it would," Bert explained. "When mankind did not understand lightning or rain, they blamed God for it. Science has not explained everything yet, but I don't want to make the same mistake the cavemen did and stick God into the equation anytime science has not had enough time to figure something out. Like Ellie said in the movie, Occam's Razor says that the simplest explanation is the right one. Now *that's* science."

"Actually, that's philosophy," Mike corrected with a wag of his finger.

"How so?" Bert challenged.

"What scientific experiment can you perform to prove Occam's Razor?" Mike asked.

"Okay, you got me. But that hardly excuses you sneaking God in where He isn't needed."

"What if something cannot be explained without God?" Mike asked. "Wouldn't Occam's Razor demand that God be part of the equation if there were no simpler theory that could explain all the evidence?"

Bert nodded, and then added, "But that isn't the case. There are plenty of theories being discussed for how the Big Bang could have happened without God. Advances in Quantum Physics, String Theory, Multiverse Scenarios . . . it's just a matter of time before they figure it out."

"I disagree," Mike said. "Do any of these theories avoid the need for a first cause beyond the natural realm?"

"Well, yeah," Bert answered, "if any of them are true, we don't need God—the universe just exists in some form or another, and that's all there is to it."

"Would that mean that the universe—in some form—has always existed?" Mike asked.

"Yes," Bert answered decisively.

"That's impossible," Mike answered, drawing incredulous looks.

"How so?" Bert asked. "And remember—no appeals to religion!"

"If the universe has always existed," Mike began, "then it has existed for an infinite amount of time. But an infinite cannot also be finite. Since we are here at the end of time, its limit in other words, the universe cannot have existed for an infinite amount of time."

There was a brief pause as Bert collected his thoughts. "I don't see the problem," he began. "We do equations with infinite numbers all the time, and they work. That's why you have microwaves and computer chips."

"Doing math with symbols for infinity is fine," Mike answered, "but infinite numbers cannot exist in reality. Once they are applied to actual quantities absurdity results. For example if you had an actual infinite number of books, and you subtracted half of them (say, the odd numbered ones), you would still have an infinite number (of even books). So infinity minus infinity is infinity. There are many problems like this, but none of them are at issue in mathematics because that deals with abstraction."

Bert thought about this for a moment. "Okay, what if there was a universe before the Big Bang or one in another dimension?"

"Would those universes have existed forever or not?" Mike asked.

"I see," Bert said. "Same problem, right?"

"As far as I can see," Mike answered.

"Wait," Bert said, "why couldn't it cause itself?"

"Nothing can cause itself. It would not have been an 'it' before it existed. That's a contradiction," Mike explained.

"Okay," Bert said, "I see where you're trying to go with this. Something else has to give the whole universe its existence. I suppose you're going to say God did it."

"We agreed not to discuss religion though," Mike reminded him with a smile, "so let's stick to philosophy for now. If there has to be something that causes all other things to exist, what sort of a being would that be?"

"An old man with a beard up in heaven?" Bert asked. Mike rolled his eyes in good humor and waited for Bert to give a better answer. "Well, it couldn't be just another created thing, so it's been around forever."

"We call that 'eternal,'" Mike said. "Would it be limited by space?"

"No, I guess not, since space is part of the universe, and it was created, too."

"So it's unlimited in presence—'omnipresent,' in other words," Mike added.

"Yeah, and super powerful and knows everything. This is starting to sound familiar," Bert laughed.

"It should," Mike said, smiling.

"And it just *happens* to be the God the Bible talks about," Bert teased. "What a shock!"

"I haven't referred to the Bible once in this discussion," Mike reminded him. "But since you insist on bringing up religion in our purely philosophical discussion, I guess I will allow it. You know, the apostle Paul said that God's invisible attributes were made obvious to all people through His creation. Perhaps this is what he was referring to."

"And I suppose Paul came up with this argument, too?" asked Bert.

"Actually, Aristotle came pretty close about four hundred years earlier," Mike reflected.

"Well, just because this argument sounds good, that doesn't mean I *have* to believe in God," concluded Bert, a little too seriously.

"You're right," Mike said, looking him in the eye. "Unfortunately, Paul said that, too."

Renee suddenly broke in. "Okay, enough philosophizing for one night; my head hurts!" Everyone laughed in agreement and started cleaning up after themselves.

On the way out, Nita said, "Mike, I was really proud of you tonight. I never could have done that—stood up to a bunch of science geeks, I mean. I guess you don't just watch movies all day, huh?" Nita joked.

"No," Mike answered her, "sometimes I watch TV."

She hit him in the arm and laughed.

CONCLUSION

Peter admonished Christians to always be ready with an answer for why they believe, and this conversation illustrates why it's a good idea to have a number of reasons for your faith that can be used in different situations. Intellectuals will probably appreciate a high-level discussion like this one more than an emotional testimony, though one's testimony can be added to, or supported by, such arguments. And Mike could have used other arguments, as well. But I wanted to illustrate how one of the more difficult arguments can be presented in an understandable way by asking questions rather than giving a lecture. This also keeps the conversation lively, friendly, and less confrontational. And remember, the discussion began with the shared experience of movie watching.

There is a big difference between belief *that* something is true and trusting *in* something as true. Someone might believe that Adolph Hitler was Germany's leader during World War II, but that would not make him a Nazi! Good arguments can help someone believe that something is true, but believing in something is a matter of the will. That is to say, it is up to the Holy Spirit to influence the will by bringing personal conviction of the truth, though He often uses good arguments in the process. Christianity does not require blind faith; it is founded on facts. Shouldn't we be compelled to share those facts with the lost?

REFLECTION QUESTIONS

1. Do you have less faith if you believe in God based on evidence?

2. How does creation reveal God's attributes (see Romans 1:20)?

3. Some have objected to using arguments for God by saying, "If someone can talk you into believing in God, then someone can also talk you out if it." Is this true? If so, is it really a problem?

DISCUSSING MOVIES SCRIPTURALLY:

Is the Bible Mythological
or Miraculous?

THE BIBLE ACCORDING TO HOLLYWOOD

CORONER:	*"What is it?"*
THOMAS:	*"Twenty-third chapter of St. John's Revelations."*
CORONER:	*"And?"*
THOMAS:	*"There is no 23rd chapter."*
CORONER:	*"Well, maybe this is the teacher's edition."* (The Prophecy)

When the Bible is used in movies, it is most often abused. Films commonly misquote references from Scripture, or even make them up entirely. One character in the 1995 film *The Prophecy* states, "Years later, of all the gospels I learned in seminary school, a verse from St. Paul stays with me. It is perhaps the strangest passage in the Bible, in which he writes, 'Even now in heaven there were angels carrying savage weapons.'" It does not take a seminarian to know that there is no such verse in the Bible. Similarly, when discussing the end of the world in *Ghostbusters* (1984), Ray Stantz cites "Revelations 7:12" concerning the opening of the sixth seal. Unfortunately, this event is recorded in chapter six, not chapter seven. A more sinister misrepresentation of Scripture takes place in *Pulp Fiction* (1994). Jules, a hit man, likes to recite Scripture to his victims, because "it [is] just a cold-blooded thing to say"–which is bad enough. Worse yet, he claims he is quoting "Ezekiel 25:17," but what he says bears little resemblance to any passage in Ezekiel–or anywhere else, for that matter.

To be fair, Hollywood does not always misuse the Bible. In *The Shaw-shank Redemption* (1994), for instance, Warden Norton correctly identifies a quotation of Mark 13:35 and Andy Dufresne recognizes John 8:12.[72] And in *Dead Man Walking* (1995), both the warden and Sister Helen cite relevant Old Testament law during their brief debate over capital punishment.

Whether the Bible is used appropriately or is unintentionally mis-handled, the fact is that in most cases the use of Scripture in a movie is seldom central to the plot. We should, however, be concerned when Hollywood intentionally undermines the authority of God's Word. This is because Christianity is based on the complete truthfulness of the Bible, not just abstract principles. If the Bible is not trustworthy, then neither is the religion founded upon it.

A hallmark of liberal theology is the assumption that the Bible can be full of myths and scientific or historical inaccuracies but still be use-ful for religion. While this is true for most other religions, it is not the case with Christianity. Jesus said in John 3:12, "I have spoken to you of earthly things and you do not believe; how then will you believe if I speak of heavenly things?" In other words, if we cannot trust Jesus with things we can verify on our own, how can we expect to trust Him for things we cannot? Thus it is important that the Bible is trustworthy in all it says, not just the "religious" parts.

The 2006 film *The Da Vinci Code* calls into question whether the Christian Bible is based on reliable sources by suggesting that the "truth" is contained in alternative gospels that the church has tried to cover up for millennia.[73] In order to answer critics who are persuaded by films such as *The Da Vinci Code*, it is important that we know why our Bible can be trusted.

HAS GOD VERIFIED HIS COMMUNICATION?

Once we have addressed the question of whether God exists, we can turn the discussion to questions about which God exists and what He has communicated. This first question can narrow down the potentially true religions considerably. If God exists, then only religions that affirm the existence of God can be true. That basically gets us down to three: Islam, Judaism, and Christianity. How do we then decide which religion adheres to the writings that are actually from the true God? Below I will show that there is a *chasm* between the Bible and all other religious writings. I use the acronym CHASM as a way to remember the evidence for the Bible. It stands for Copies, History, Archeology, Science, and Miracles. The first four establish that the Bible we have today is trustworthy, the last one shows that it is, like Jesus, both human and divine in nature.

Copies

One common objection to the trustworthiness of the Bible goes like this: Because the Bible we have today is a translation of a translation of a translation, we don't really know what the original Bible said. This is simply false. The copy evidence for the Bible is, in a word, astounding. We have more manuscripts, better manuscripts, and earlier manuscripts of the Bible than of any other ancient writing.

In the case of the Old Testament, the oldest manuscripts we had access to for many years dated back to about the fourteenth century AD. For centuries, these were the oldest copies translators had to work with. That all changed in 1948. In that year, shepherds discovered the Dead Sea Scrolls in the caves of Qumran, which date back to the third century BC. This amazing discovery included the entire book of Isaiah and thousands of fragments from every Old Testament book except Esther. This gave scholars access to copies nearly two thousand years older than their current manuscripts and verified the incredible accuracy of scribal copying.[74]

When it comes to the New Testament, we can be confident we are reading from accurate sources, because we have so many ancient copies to compare. For many ancient texts there are only a handful of manuscripts in existence.

We have only nine or ten good copies of Julius Caesar's *The Gallic Wars.* The best-preserved, non-biblical ancient writing we have is Homer's *Iliad,* of which there are only 643 copies. Compare these numbers to the New Testament, which is based on nearly six thousand Greek manuscripts plus over nine thousand ancient copies in other languages. If that were not enough, even if all of these copies were lost, we could reconstruct all but eleven verses of the New Testament from ancient quotations of the Bible.

Furthermore, we also have much earlier copies of the Bible than most ancient writings. While some of the earliest copies of non-biblical writings date to thousands of years later than their originals (Homer's *Odyssey* is unusually good; only five hundred years separate the copies from the original), we have fragments of the New Testament that date to within decades of the events they record. This does not allow enough time for distortion or myth making.

Finally, we have more accurate copies of the Bible than of most other ancient texts. Because there are over thirty-six thousand verses in the New Testament, we might expect there to be hundreds of thousands of variations between the many existing manuscripts. Instead, there is a total difference of only about 2 percent. Very few of these variants affect the meaning of the passage—for instance, manuscripts vary in their use of "Christ," "Jesus Christ," and "Jesus"—and none of these variations affect any area of doctrine. Obviously, God preserved His Word as it was copied and transmitted.[75]

History

Although the Bible is itself a collection of historical documents, it would be appropriate to doubt their veracity if no other historical sources verified what it said. It would be reasonable a hundred years from now, for instance, to doubt that the tragic events of September 11, 2001, ever took place if no newspaper or television news stations ever reported on them. However, many historians of the day recorded the same events reported in the New Testament, and most of the gospel itself can be reconstructed from non-Christian sources:

- **Tacitus** (first-century Roman historian) makes references to Christians suffering under Pontius Pilate during the reign of Tiberius. He also records a "superstition" relating to the resurrection of Jesus.

- **Suetonius** (first-century Roman historian and biographer of the Caesars) records that there was a man named *Chrestus* (or Christ) who lived during the first century. Certain Jews caused disturbances relating to this man.

- **Flavius Josephus** (first-century Jewish historian) refers to James, "the brother of Jesus, who was called Christ." He also wrote that "there was a wise man named Jesus. His conduct was good and [he] was known to be virtuous. And many people from among the Jews and the other nations became his disciples. Pilate condemned him to be crucified and to die. But those who became his disciples did not abandon his discipleship. They reported that he had appeared to them three days after his crucifixion, and that he was alive; accordingly he was perhaps the Messiah, concerning whom the prophets have recounted wonders."

- **Thallus** (first-century Roman historian) discusses darkness and earthquakes that Julius Africanus (third-century historian) says followed the crucifixion, as described in Luke 23:44-45.

- **Pliny the Younger** (an early second-century Roman senator) describes early Christian worship practices, most notably that early Christians worshiped Jesus as God.

- **The Talmud** (a collection of Jewish Rabbinic teachings and history) confirms Jesus' crucifixion, the timing of the event on the eve of Passover, and records accusations against Jesus of sorcery and apostasy.[76]

From these sources alone we can conclude that Jesus lived a virtuous life, performed miracles, was crucified during Passover in Palestine under Pontius Pilate during the reign of Tiberius, that His disciples believed Him to have been miraculously resurrected, and that they worshiped Him as God.

Archeology

History is replete with archeological evidence for the veracity of the Old Testament. It also records many stories of how more recent discoveries have overthrown theories that attacked the Old Testament account. One example is the discovery of the Hittite civilization, first mentioned in Genesis 10:15, in 1906. Similarly, after centuries of scoffing, archeologists confirmed that Daniel had accurately recorded Belshazzar's position as co-regent—something only an eyewitness would have known (Daniel 5:16). Archeologists have even confirmed that the city of Tyre was destroyed by Nebuchadnezzar of Babylon and, later, Alexander the Great, in exactly the way the prophet Ezekiel predicted.[77]

There is similar evidence for the veracity of the New Testament. In fact, the evidence is so strong that it converted a skeptic named Sir William Ramsay, who had originally set out to disprove Luke's account in the book of Acts. He was amazed to find that Luke's abilities as a historian were unsurpassed.[78] Similarly, archeologist William F. Albright gave up his skeptical views on Scripture when he found archeological evidence supporting the literal accuracy of the New Testament.[79] Historian A. N. Sherwin-White concluded that "for Acts, the confirmation of historicity is overwhelming. . . . Any attempt to reject its basic historicity must now appear absurd."[80]

Science

It may be hard to believe today, but science has long been a friend of the Bible. In fact, many of the greatest scientists of all time have been Bible-believing Christians, including Roger Bacon, Johannes Kepler, Blaise Pascal, Robert Boyle, and Gregor Mendel.[81] Many people today have been confused about the Bible's reliability due to claims that science has disproved what it says. But in fact, science has never proven the Bible incorrect.

The scientific accuracy of the Bible is astonishing, if one considers when it was written. For instance, one of the oldest books in the Bible proclaimed the earth to be round (Job 26:10). The writings of Isaiah (around 800 BC) include a similar description (Isaiah 40:22). This not only shows the Bible's trustworthiness but also implies a divine rather than human origin. The following are additional scientific facts known to biblical writers long before they were studied by science:

- The earth is suspended in space by nothing (Job 26:7).
- Man is made up of the basic elements of the earth (Genesis 2:7).
- Life is found in the blood (Genesis 9:4; Leviticus 17:14).
- The movements of the winds (Ecclesiastes 1:6).
- The water cycle (Job 28:25-26; Ecclesiastes 1:7)
- The law of increasing entropy (Psalm 102:25-27)

One of the biggest issues between the Bible and science today is, of course, the theory of evolution. Space does not permit a detailed look at the current arguments over this theory, but it is important to know that, contrary to what Hollywood and most media outlets assume, the issue is far from settled.[82] For our purposes, simply bear in mind that science has not made confidence in the Scriptures naïve or irrational.

THE BIBLE IS INSPIRED

Miracles

Perhaps the most important evidence for the truth of the Bible is its inspiration by God. After all, any book can claim divine truth, and simply being historically correct and accurately copied does not indicate divine authorship. There are many books that could pass the tests of historicity and scientific validity. But whether or not the Bible is actually ultimate in its truth does not hinge on these prior proofs. The real confirmation of the Bible's claim to divine truth is in its miracles. Although these come in several types, here we'll focus on two.

Prophecy

As early as Justin Martyr in the second century, Christian apologists have appealed to fulfilled prophecy as miraculous proof for the truth of Christianity. Blaise Pascal, the brilliant seventeenth-century mathematician, wrote in *Pensée* 693:

I see many contradictory religions, and consequently all false save

one. Each wants to be believed on its own authority, and threatens
unbelievers. I do not therefore believe them. Every one can say
this; every one can call himself a prophet. But I see that Christian
religion wherein prophecies are fulfilled; and that is what every one
cannot do.[83]

God used prophets to proclaim and write down His Word. Further, God used fulfilled prophecy to authenticate these messengers: "You may say to yourselves, 'How can we know when a message has not been spoken by the Lord?' If what a prophet proclaims in the name of the Lord does not take place or come true, that is a message the Lord has not spoken. That prophet has spoken presumptuously" (Deuteronomy 18:21-22; see also Isaiah 41:21-23). The question before us now is, "Does the Bible contain predictive prophecy to authenticate its message?" Absolutely.

The book of Daniel predicted with perfect accuracy the coming of the four great kingdoms from Babylon to Rome. Details concerning how they would rule and fall were recorded centuries before any of those events took place. So precise are these prophecies that even critics agree that Daniel wrote accurately. They simply try to avoid the implication of supernatural involvement by claiming these words are actually evidence that Daniel wrote after the fact!

Ezekiel 26 records in astonishing detail how the city of Tyre was to be destroyed, how it would be torn down, and how its debris would be thrown into the sea. When Alexander the Great marched on that area in 332 BC, he encountered a group of people holed up in a tower on an island off the coast. Because he could not cross the sea, he could not attack the tower. Rather than wait them out, the proud conqueror had his army throw stones into the sea to build a land bridge to the tower. It worked. His army crossed the sea and overthrew the occupants of the stronghold. But where did he get so much stone? The rocks used for the land bridge were rubble from the city of Tyre. Its stones were cast into the sea exactly as Ezekiel had prophesied centuries earlier![84]

Furthermore, there are so many prophecies concerning Christ in the Old

Testament (over 270) that it would take several pages to list them all. They include the time and place of His birth (Daniel 9:25; Micah 5:2), and His ancestry (Genesis 49:10). These specifications alone narrow Christ's identity down to only a few possible individuals in all of human history. Prophecies concerning Jesus' death were likewise made centuries in advance, even before crucifixion was developed as a method of execution. These include the piercing of His hands and feet, the piercing of His side, and the casting of lots for His garments.[85] The odds of one man accidentally fulfilling even sixteen of these prophecies have been calculated to be 1 in 10,000,000,000,000,000, 000,000,000,000,000,000,000,000,000,000 (a quattuordecillion)!

Jesus Himself made several prophecies. Among the most dramatic were those concerning the fall of Jerusalem and the destruction of the temple. Jesus predicted the signs that would precede this event, including that believers would be saved by fleeing the city, and that this would all occur within one generation.[86] This was fulfilled in AD 70 when the Romans laid siege to the city and burned the temple to its foundation.

The Resurrection of Jesus Christ

ALADDIN: | *"Some all-powerful genie! Can't even bring people back from the dead!"* (Aladdin)

Besides numerous healings and nature miracles, Jesus Christ demonstrated His authority and deity primarily through the miracle of His resurrection. Many historical facts surround the Resurrection that most scholars, even skeptical ones, agree are true. Alternate theories have been put forth to explain away these historical facts, but none of them can account for all the data. Such theories include claims that Jesus only fainted and merely appeared to die, that someone stole His body, that He was buried in a common graveyard, or that His appearances were hallucinations. The following are some quick rebuttals to these common objections:

1. Jesus' death was real. We know from medical science and the nature of

crucifixion that the idea that He only fainted is false.

2. Jesus' tomb was found empty, which would not be explained by hallucinations.

3. Jesus' appearances were reported by many people—even His enemies. This rules out the stolen body or common grave theories.

4. Jesus' disciples went from hiding in fright to boldly proclaiming the truth of Christianity, because of what they knew to be true. Many died horrible deaths because they would not recant their message of Jesus' resurrection. Some people will die for what they believe is true, but no one will die for what they know is false.[87]

In 1 Corinthians 15:3-8, Paul provides a solid defense of Jesus' resurrection. Paul says that Jesus was buried (proving that He was dead), was raised (proving that He was who He claimed to be), and appeared to hundreds of people—both believers and skeptics—as proof that it all occurred. As it turns out, Christ's resurrection is the strongest positive case for the gospel, when it could have been the strongest case against it. If Christ's resurrection did not take place, then faith in the gospel is in vain and we might as well "party down," for death is all that awaits us! No other religion binds itself to verifiable evidence in this way. First Corinthians 15 was one of the earliest writings of the Christian church, written at a time when the resurrection was being preached as the reason for the Christian's hope. For Paul to stake Christianity's truthfulness on Christ's resurrection at a time when it could have easily been disproved shows how strong a case there was for it.

As the apostle Peter wrote, "We did not follow cunningly devised fables when we made known to you the power and coming of our Lord Jesus Christ, but we were eyewitnesses of his majesty" (2 Peter 1:16 NKJV). The followers of Jesus Christ were not members of some starry-eyed, gullible fan club. They were witnesses to His miracles. Jesus Christ's resurrection transformed the disciples from timid, scared men into super-missionaries and became the backbone of the gospel message that spread throughout the world. "So then, dear brothers and sisters, be firm. Do not be moved! Always be outstanding in the work of the Lord, knowing that your labor is not in vain in the Lord."[88]

Coffee Shop Talk:

A DATE, WITH *THE DA VINCI CODE*

Nita and Mike had continued dating throughout the semester. Renee and Bert were also growing quite close, and the two couples often went out together. When the semester finally drew to a close, the four friends were in their favorite corner of Café Veritas celebrating the coming break and spending the money they made selling their old textbooks.

"Well, you two have become quite the little couple," Renee said, grinning at Mike and Nita. "After that first date, I thought you'd never make it!"

"Well," said Mike, "she finally wore me down." This brought laughter and knowing glances between the girls.

"Does this mean the relationship will last beyond the confines of Fall semester?" Renee asked.

"Give them a break," Bert said. "It's not like they're going to get married or anything." At this, Mike and Nita both tried to hide grins, but they did not escape Bert's notice. "Right?" he asked.

"Well . . ." Nita began.

"Oh, my gosh!" exclaimed Renee. "You had better not have gotten engaged without telling us!"

"No, no. Nothing like that," explained Nita. "But I won't say we haven't been talking about it." She squeezed closer to Mike.

"Get a room," Bert said happily, then raised his eyebrows toward Renee.

"Don't even think about it, buddy," she said menacingly. "Speaking of marriages, Bert and I saw *The Da Vinci Code* this weekend."

Mike groaned inwardly. He had been dealing with *Da Vinci*

Code-related questions for months after the book became such a huge seller. He had read the book and actually enjoyed it, for the most part. But he knew the controversial material was what Renee was interested in. He decided to go with the flow and asked, "What did you think?"

"We both liked the book better, but the movie was fun," Renee answered for both of them. "One interesting thing though—in the book the hero, Langdon, and the historian, Teabing, are completely in agreement with one another and we are never given even a taste of contrary evidence or opposing theories. In the movie, however, Langdon is somewhat skeptical of the whole Grail legend. Further, Teabing is not portrayed as a master historian in the movie, but more of an eccentric old rich guy. At the end of the film, however, there's this dramatic conversion experience with Langdon kneeling before Mary Magdalene's tomb."

"It sounds like the film starts out as slightly more balanced between truth and error, but ends affirming the error more than the book," Mike mused.

"It's just a movie, Mike," Bert said. "Don't take it so seriously."

Mike looked up, surprised to still be hearing this objection after all this time. "Well, the problem is that although the *Da Vinci Code* story is put forth as fictional, its background is not. People ignorant of the subject matter cannot tell the difference between the fictional foreground and the equally fictional background elements. The things he puts forth as fact are a joke; virtually nothing in Brown's conspiracy theory is taken seriously, even by liberal historians."

"Like what, Mike?" asked Renee.

"Like the idea that the Bible has evolved through, and been corrupted by, countless translations, additions, and revisions," Mike began. "This subject has been covered so comprehensively that

Brown's misrepresentation of the facts is inexcusable. Knowledge-able textual critics would never make such assertions. If we throw out the Bible, we should be consistent and throw out all of ancient history, for none of it is recorded with more accuracy and multiplicity than the Bible. When you look at the manuscripts, historical evidence, archeology . . ."

Bert interrupted before Mike could continue. "What about all the other gospels that were considered for the New Testament before it was finally collected by Constantine?" asked Bert.

"Also false," answered Mike. "There were very few books of the New Testament that were involved in any dispute. The Church collected the manuscripts and accepted them as they went along. Councils convened when heretical disputes arose, but Constantine had nothing to do with it. The question about which books to include was not handled through the sort of process *The Da Vinci Code* alludes to—as if there were all these comparable works lying around and one or a few men simply picked their favorites. There was near universal acceptance of the four canonical Gospels—Matthew, Mark, Luke, and John—by the middle of the second century. None of the non-canonical gospels were even close in date of composition, breadth of distribution, or proportion of acceptance. As for the Coptic Scrolls found at Nag Hammadi, which *The Da Vinci Code* mentions elsewhere, these are heretical Gnostic writings that were not even around when the canon of Scripture was formed. *The Da Vinci Code* also makes no mention of the most famous Gnostic gospel, The Gospel of Thomas. There's a good reason for that: it ends with an admonition that women must 'become male' in order to find salvation! Needless to say, this would not fit Brown's agenda of promoting the 'feminine divine.'"

"Someone's been doing some studying!" Renee said, shocked and impressed with Mike's knowledge of the subject.

"To quote the smartest man on earth," Mike replied, "'Just wait 'til I get going!'"

Bert looked perplexed.

"It's from *The Princess Bride*, you cultural ignoramus," Renee scolded him.

They all laughed and then Mike continued. "The same goes for *The Da Vinci Code* claims regarding Jesus. Jesus' claims to deity, and His supernatural activity to prove those claims, are thoroughly obvious in the earliest and best documents about His life. In fact, the earliest heresies were those that made Jesus out to be *merely* deity! The Council of Nicaea was not formed to stop a Christian war that threatened to tear the empire apart. Christian persecution had only recently been stopped! Nor was Christ's deity a 'close call,' as *The Da Vinci Code* states. Only two out of three hundred bishops at the Council did not sign the statement affirming the full deity of Christ. Moreover, the fact that *The Da Vinci Code* states that Jesus' having a child would 'bring the church to its knees' betrays a serious misunderstanding regarding Jesus' nature—or rather, *natures*. There is no problem in affirming that Jesus, as a full human being, could procreate. I think the pragmatic problems resulting from Christ's having an 'heir,' so to speak, probably kept it from happening, but it would in no way threaten His divine nature any more than His rising from the dead threatened His human nature."

"So what about His marriage to Mary Magdalene?" Renee asked winking at Nita who just smiled and shook her head.

"This is another area where *The Da Vinci Code* goes wrong. Nothing in the New Testament or any other 'gospel' asserts that Jesus was married. *The Da Vinci Code* is committing the classic fallacy of arguing from ignorance. We should not affirm something as proved simply because it is not specifically denied. Mary Magdalene is never referenced with any special notice in Scripture, and her title, which lacks reference to a husband, shows that she was not married."

"But the book says that the royal bloodline of Jesus Christ has been established by scores of historians," Bert said. "That *must* make it true." He grinned knowing that this was probably not the case.

Mike groaned. "There were only four people listed in the book, and not one has an academic degree in history."

"Well, I enjoyed it," Renee said, "even if it is false."

At this, Nita chimed in. "Sure, everyone loves a good conspiracy theory, but *The Da Vinci Code* makes for a bigger problem. Many people are forming their opinions about art, history, Jesus, and Christianity based on this fictional novel. Faulty history and silly opinions about art are one thing, but lies about Jesus Christ are another. If someone is going to hell because of unbelief, they should at least have good reasons!" An uncomfortable silence followed. "Sorry," she said, "I didn't mean to . . ."

Renee cut her off. "Don't apologize, Nita," she admonished. "If what you believe is true, then it would be awful of you not to tell others." She leaned in closer. "Bert and I have been reading that book you guys gave us last month, and I have to admit it is pretty convincing."

"Really?" Nita asked, "Oh Renee, that's great!"

"Well, we're not ready to sign on the dotted line yet," explained Bert, "but we appreciate you guys taking the time to talk to us like real people and not just religious projects."

The two couples finished their tea, returned the mugs to the counter, and hugged good-bye. Back outside, as Bert and Renee drove back to the campus, Nita and Mike talked about what Renee had said.

"Do you think they will become Christians?" Nita asked Mike.

"I don't know," he answered, "but we have fulfilled our duty as believers and friends. We explained the problem, offered the solution, and answered their questions. Fortunately for us, that's all we're responsible for doing."

"The rest is up to God," said Nita. Mike nodded in response and looked down at her. She looked up at him, gave him a quick kiss, and then, with a sassy expression on her face, asked, "So, you want to go catch a movie?"

CONCLUSION

Attacks against the Bible are not merely historical issues; they strike at the heart of the Christian message. Christianity, unlike almost all other religions, has made claims that are testable. It's not just a collection of proverbs or a life philosophy. Christianity is a historical faith rooted in historical events. Take away Buddha, and you can still have Buddhism. But take away a risen Christ, and Christianity is a sham (remember 1 Corinthians 15:13-19). The truth of the gospel message is dependent upon the reliability of the Scriptures that communicate it. How many other religions open themselves up to this kind of investigation?

The Bible we have today is trustworthy in all it affirms, for we have accurate copies that agree with known history, as confirmed by archeology, and it is not at odds with scientific facts. Most importantly, it is the only religious writing that has the divine seal of authority: supernatural miracles and prophecy. For this reason, we have no excuse for ignoring God's testimony about Himself.

REFLECTION QUESTIONS

1. Should Christians pray about whether or not a religious teaching is really from God (see Deuteronomy chapters 13 and 18)?

2. Is there good evidence that the Bible is God's Word and not just another religious writing?

3. If it were proved that Jesus did not really die and rise again, would it exhibit more faith to be a Christian anyway (see 1 Corinthians 15:12-20)?

ACT THREE

APPLAUDING & AVOIDING MOVIES

ACT THREE

APPLAUDING & AVOIDING MOVIES

What Should We Then Watch?

CHRISTIANS AT THE MOVIES

As has been mentioned throughout this book, not every movie is appropriate for every viewer. It's one thing to deem a movie "good" by objective cinematic standards. It takes different criteria to determine whether you should watch a given movie yourself or recommend it to your friends and family.

Ultimately, that decision is a personal one. Nevertheless, Christians often feel a great deal of pressure from one another regarding how they choose their entertainment. As we near the book's end, I would like to discuss some principles regarding the Christian's relationship with movie viewing in general that can be applied to choosing which movies to watch in particular.

BIBLICAL ENTERTAINMENT STANDARDS

Some people think that the Bible is against having fun. While the Bible does warn against seeking pleasure just to avoid more important things in life (Jeremiah 15:17; Luke 8:14; James 4:8-10), one of the wisest people in the world, King Solomon, said that having fun once in a while is good for easing the strain of a life of hard work (Ecclesiastes 8:15). Movies can provide enjoyable entertainment, but they can also distract us from more important things. So first we must make sure we have our priorities straight (Ephesians 5:15-21).

Next, we need to make sure that our entertainment choices are biblical ones. While we may watch movies for a variety of reasons, when watching movies for entertainment, we should seek movies whose enjoyment is glorifying to God (1 Corinthians 10:31). Because we are affected by what we spend time around (Psalm 1:1; Proverbs 6:27; 1 Corinthians 15:33), we need to be sure that our entertainment will not lead to negative consequences for ourselves (1 Corinthians 10:23), or others (1 Corinthians 9; Romans 14).

What constitutes a biblical choice of movies to enjoy? Philippians 4:8 (NASB) lists several considerations that can safeguard your choices: "Whatever is true, whatever is honorable, whatever is right, whatever is pure, whatever is lovely, whatever is of good repute, if there is any excellence and if anything worthy of praise, dwell on these things." Because movies have such a strong impact on us (if they didn't we wouldn't watch them), we need to be careful that we do not set ourselves up to dwell on what is negative or inappropriate.

AVOIDING THE APPEARANCE OF EVIL

However, many Christians have developed a mistaken understanding of biblical morality based on a misinterpretation of First Thessalonians 5:22. In the King James Version of the Bible this verse reads, "Abstain from all appearance of evil." However, the text is more properly rendered, "Stay away from every form of evil."[89] First Thessalonians 5:21 (NASB) says that we are to "examine everything carefully [and] hold fast to that which is good." This positive charge is followed and reinforced by the injunction to avoid that which is evil (no matter what it looks like). There is nothing here about avoiding bars, movie theaters, or sinners in order to avoid being perceived as sinful. We can't be responsible for how others judge our motives when we perform actions that are not sinful (*now* is the proper time to quote Matthew 7:1!).

Both Jesus and Paul provide biblical examples of how someone can participate in cultural activities without sinning. Jesus was known for irritating the religious establishment by hanging out with the "wrong crowd" and breaking some traditional, but man-made, rules,[90] yet He never sinned.[91] Paul said he became all things to all men, meaning that he changed his behavior in ways that would help him best fit in with those to whom he was witnessing

(1 Corinthians 9:22). He was a "Jew to the Jews" and a "Gentile to the Gentiles." When he spoke with Jews, for instance, he referred them to the Scriptures (Acts 17:2); but when he dealt with Gentiles, he referred to their own writers (Acts 17:22-34). He adapted to the culture as much as possible without over-stepping biblical morality (e.g., Acts 16:3; cf. 1 Corinthians 7:18-19).

Both Jesus and Paul were free to act as they thought best when they were dealing with non-moral issues. The "appearance of evil" was not a concern. So what does this have to do with movie watching? Because many movies promote sinful lifestyles, some Christians have been taught that movie viewing is evil–period. Thus, even entering a movie theater would appear to be evil. Yet to avoid all movies because of the bad ones is difficult to justify biblically. Movies are just stories told through "moving pictures," and the Bible is certainly not against stories. Of course these examples of cultural engagement in Scripture do not overthrow exhortations against sinning in the process.

"IN" THE WORLD BUT NOT "OF" IT

In Christian circles, "the world" often refers neither to planet Earth nor to its population of humans. Instead, in the context of righteous living, "the world" connotes the sinful system we find ourselves in.

Jesus says Christians are no longer *of* this world, but we are to remain *in* it (John 17:6-20). We are to be set apart. Does that mean we should restrict ourselves to participating only in "Christian" groups and activities, attending only "Christian" movies, or listening only to "Christian" music? Certainly not. Just as Jesus was sent into the world but was never "of it," so He sends us out to be in the world but not "of it." How Jesus lived His life while in the world is our model. As we discover from Jesus' example, there is an important difference between doing things that people do in the world and doing worldly things.

When trying to determine whether a certain behavior is "worldly," it does us no good to simply point out that "the world does it." The world uses ballpoint pens, breathes air, and wears blue jeans. Sinners can do things that aren't sinful. So too we can share in many of the world's activities without participating in them in a worldly way. The issue is whether we are doing things according to the sinful nature of the world or according to our new nature as believers (Ephesians 2:1-10).

Further, we must avoid sinning, but this does not mean avoiding *sinners*. We can be friends with people in the world without being friends of the world. Seeking to understand the world's mind-set does not mean we have to attain the world's mind. Thus, understanding the difference between "in" and "of" is the key to avoiding sinful compromise without succumbing to sinful isolationism.

This might mean that some Christians will need to avoid things that appeal to their flesh, and this means being honest about motives. We should never use cultural relevancy as an excuse to give in to the flesh. We must know our limits and the areas in which we struggle, and make our choices accordingly.

I would advise you to check a movie's reviews before making plans to watch it with others. That will save you the embarrassment of walking out of a movie when you are surprised by questionable material. But, by all means, walk out if you must. There is nothing wrong with acting according to your morals. If anyone asks, just be honest and tell them you're not comfortable with the film, and where you will meet them when the movie is over. This way you are not backing out of the plans you have made, they don't have to worry that you are offended, and your witness is not tarnished by a condescending attitude. If your friends are Christians, make sure your judgment of those who stay in the movie does not cross the line into legalistic false piety. Remember that not everyone shares your struggles. If you think the film was objectively sinful to watch, then you should discuss that later with a view toward discipleship, not discipline. If you went with non-Christians, then don't make an issue of it unless you can bring about a constructive conversation. Your job is not to convert your friends to Christian morality, but to influence them to come to Christ. He'll take care of the rest.

STRONGER AND WEAKER CHRISTIANS

There is also a lot of confusion in the Christian subculture regarding those whom the apostle Paul refers to as "strong" and "weak" believers.[92] Christians often view more conservative believers as stronger—or at least more spiritual—but the opposite is often the case. Paul defines the stronger believer as the one who rightly judges activities as moral (and thus desirable), immoral (and thus to be avoided), or non-moral (and therefore matters of freedom). The weaker believer often puts non-moral things into the "immoral" category.

When Paul wrote his first letter to the Corinthians, Christians there were struggling to understand how to think about eating food that had been sacrificed to idols. Some correctly believed it was okay to eat such food because "an idol is nothing," and could not, therefore, actually do anything to the food. Paul describes those who believed that the food had become evil somehow as suffering from weak consciences due to ignorance. They thought they knew the truth of the situation but "did not yet know to the degree that they needed to know." Paul indicated that this situation was technically a non-moral issue, for the people "would be no worse if they did not eat and no better if they did." In other words, the weaker, more "conservative" believers were mistaken. They were more conservative only in the sense that they participated in fewer activities, not because they were less sinful.

Several problems can arise from confusion over this issue. First, the weaker believer may become judgmental of others, either stronger believers or unbelievers, who behave in ways that they wrongly consider to be immoral. Conversely, the strong believer may judge the weaker for their naiveté. Yet the stronger brother is not right for judging the weaker even though the weaker brother is in error, and the weaker is not right (nor more spiritual) when he judges the stronger for his liberty. In non-moral matters, both are accountable to God alone.

Another possibility is that the stronger believer may cause the weaker to stumble because of his or her actions.[93] "Stumbling" is another term that is often misunderstood. Strong believers are those who "possess knowledge" that has cleared their conscience and given them the liberty to act accordingly. A stumbling problem arises if a weaker believer sees the stronger acting in a way that the weaker mistakenly believes is sinful and decides to participate in the behavior based solely on the stronger believer's actions. Paul says that it is sinful for the weaker Christian to act against his conscience. For this reason, he commands the stronger believer not to behave in a way that will cause weaker believers to stumble in their actions.

What this means is that just because one believer does not like what another is doing, the first believer is not necessarily in danger of stumbling. There will always be people who have issues with nearly every action, so the only way to solve every potential stumbling problem would be to stop doing anything! After all, Jesus drank wine and John the Baptist did not, yet they were both accused of sin (Luke 7:33-35). Rather, true stumbling is knowingly causing weaker believers to act against their consciences even though what they are doing is not sinful in itself.

Furthermore, stronger believers are not expected to pretend that they agree with weaker believers, nor are they to affirm them in their error. Paul says the stronger should not allow the weaker to speak evil of that which is not evil. He simply instructs them not to partake in the behavior in question in front of the weaker person, if it might cause them to join in and go against their conscience. But at some point the weaker believers will have to be confronted with their error or they will never mature and grow stronger in truth.[94] Thus teaching someone the truth about the ethical status of a given activity is not the same thing as performing the action in front of them.

In areas of legitimate dispute, we must exercise charity. Not an unbiblical charity that keeps mature believers in bondage to immature viewpoints, or that merely tolerates so-called "worldly believers" who engage in activities that other Christians find questionable, but charity that recognizes all of these people as full brothers and sisters in Christ. If Christians are going to act in unity, we need to debate these issues but not divide over them. Tensions resulting from the clash of opinions on non-moral issues will be with us until Jesus returns. In the meantime we need to allow each other freedom of conscience in disputable areas—including movie choices—while sharing our honest opinions with each other in a loving manner.

FINAL WORDS

I sincerely hope that this book has helped you become a more thoughtful movie watcher and has equipped you to use movies as a way of engaging your non-Christian friends with the gospel. I also hope that once you have internalized these basic principles, you will add to this working script and make it your own. As we have seen, movies provide ample opportunity to engage in conversation that leads to the gospel. To make the most of movies, then, keep the following principles in mind:

1. Watch and enjoy movies for what they are before you begin your evaluations.

2. Distinctly evaluate the style, story, suppositions, and message of the films you watch.

3. Note any features that stand out as conversation points in each film (including biblical, theological, and philosophical issues).

4. Prepare yourself to defend the Christian worldview in areas where the film suggests an alternative worldview.

5. Bring up the film in conversation and ask questions that lead deeper into the film's message so you can share the gospel when appropriate.

I hope this book has given you the tools and direction you need to increase your enjoyment of film. More importantly, I hope you feel better equipped to use films as a way to make your proclamation and defense of the faith even more relevant to the lost today.

REFLECTION QUESTIONS

1. What is the best way to handle a fellow Christian who disagrees with your ethics concerning movie viewing?

2. If you knew someone was coming to your house who did not think Christians should ever watch R-rated movies, and you had some in your collection, should you hide them?

3. What should you do to make sure your motives are right when watching any movie?

ROLL CREDITS . . .

CREW

Writer/Director	Douglas M. Beaumont
Executive Producers	Steve Lyon and Paul Santhouse
Line Producer	Madison Trammel
Editor	Christopher Reese
Production Assistant	Nathan Pierce
Director of Photography	Delayna Kenney
Continuity Consultant	Lanny Wilson
Pre-Production Editor	Christina Woodside
Set Manager	Elaine Beaumont
Best Boy	Michael Philip
Gaffers	Mike and Donna Beaumont
Key Grip	Joyce Peterson
Matte Artists	Brian and Connie McElhany
Stunts	Leroy and Janelle Lamar
Musical Direction	Matt and Kristin Barclay
Pyrotechnician	Eric Vözzy
Runner	Ben Dresser
Props/Costumes	Matt and Jill Graham
Foley Artists	Brandon and Andrea Dahm
Negative Cutters	Phil and Gini Hoff
Special Effects	Jason Reed
Choreographer	Richard Howe
Background Artist	Sonny Fleming

The characters and incidents portrayed, and the names used herein, are fictitious. Any resemblance to the names, character, or history of any person is coincidental and unintentional. Except where it's not.

SPEAKING OF MOVIES . . .

Doug is available to speak on movies, music, apologetics, theology, and a host of other interesting topics, so please do not hesitate to visit his Web site if you would be interested in having him speak at your event.

www.DougBeaumont.org

or

www.MessageBehindTheMovie.com

RESOURCES ON FILM, CULTURE, AND CHRISTIANITY

Here is a list of works that have been helpful to me in the preparation of this book (whether I fully agree with them or not).

Art, Film, Story, and Culture

Abanes, Richard. *Fantasy and Your Family: A Closer Look at The Lord of the Rings, Harry Potter, and Magick in the Modern World.* Camp Hill, PA: Christian Publications: 2002.

——. *The Truth Behind the Da Vinci Code.* Eugene, OR: Harvest House Publishers, 2004.

Anderson, Philip Longfellow. *The Gospel in Disney: Christian Values in the Early Animated Classics.* Minneapolis: Augsburg Books, 2004.

Baehr, Ted and Pat Boone. *The Culture-Wise Family.* Ventura, CA: Regal, 2007.

Barsotti, Catherine M. and Robert K. Johnston. *Finding God in the Movies.* Grand Rapids, MI: Baker Books, 2004.

Boggs, Joseph M. and Dennis W. Petrie. *The Art of Watching Films.* 7th ed. Boston: McGraw Hill, 2008.

Bordwell, David and Kristin Thompson. *Film Art: An Introduction.* 8th ed. Boston: McGraw Hill, 2008.

Bortolin, Matthew. *The Dharma of Star Wars.* Boston: Wisdom Publications, 2005.

Brown, Nancy Carpentier. *The Mystery of Harry Potter.* Huntington, IN: Our Sunday Visitor Publishing, 2007.

Buckland, Warren. *Film Studies.* London: Hodder and Stoughton, 1998.

Burns, Kevin [Director]. *Playboy Presents Sex at 24 Frames per Second: The Ultimate Journey Through Sex in Cinema* [Documentary Film]. Prometheus Entertainment: 2003.

Campbell, Joseph. *The Hero with a Thousand Faces.* 2nd ed. Princeton, NJ: Princeton University Press, 1973.

Campbell, Joseph with Bill Moyers. *The Power of Myth*. Betty Sue Flowers, ed. New York: Anchor Books-Doubleday, 1988.

Clover, Joshua. *The Matrix*. London: British Film Institute, 2004.

Comfort, Ray. *Hollywood Be Thy Name*. Orlando, FL: Bridge-Logos, 2007.

——. *What Hollywood Believes*. Bartlesville, OK: Genesis Publishing Group, 2004.

Decker, Kevin and Jason T. Eberl. *Star Wars and Philosophy*. La Salle, IL: Open Court, 2005.

Detweiler, Craig. *Into the Dark: Seeing the Sacred in the Top Films of the 21st Century*. Grand Rapids, MI: Baker Academic, 2008.

Dyer, Richard. *Seven*. London: British Film Institute, 2005.

Eco, Umberto. *The Aesthetics of Thomas Aquinas*. Tr. Hugh Bredin. Cambridge, MA: Harvard University Press, 1988.

Elsaesser, Thomas and Warren Buckland. *Studying Contemporary American Film: A Guide to Movie Analysis*. New York: Oxford University Press, 2002.

Field, Syd. *Screenplay: The Foundations of Screenwriting*. 3rd ed. New York: Bantam Doubleday Dell, 1994.

Geisler, Norman and J. Yutaka Amano. *Religion of the Force*. Dallas: Quest Publications, 1983.

Geivett, R. Douglas and James S. Spiegel, eds. *Faith, Film and Philosophy: Big Ideas on the Big Screen*. Downers Grove, IL: IVP Academic, 2007.

Giannetti, Louis. *Understanding Movies*. 6th ed. Upper Saddle River, NJ: Prentice Hall, 1993.

Gilson, Etienne. *The Arts of the Beautiful*. Champaign, IL: Dalkey Archive Press, 2000.

——. *Forms and Substances in the Arts*. Tr. Salvator Attansio. Champaign, IL: Dalkey Archive Press, 2001.

Godawa, Brian. *Hollywood Worldviews: Watching Films with Wisdom and Discernment*. Downers Grove, IL: InterVarsity Press, 2002.

Hibbs, Thomas S. *Shows About Nothing: Nihilism in Popular Culture from The Exorcist to Seinfeld*. Dallas: Spence Publishing Company, 1999.

Hofstadter, Albert and Richard Kuhns. *Philosophies of Art and Beauty*. Chicago: University of Chicago Press, 1976.

Johnston, Robert K. *Reel Spirituality: Theology and Film in Dialogue*. Grand Rapids, MI: Baker Academic, 2000.

——, ed. *Reframing Theology and Film: New Focus for an Emerging Discipline*. Grand Rapids, MI: Baker Academic, 2007.

Kermode, Mark. *The Exorcist*. Rev. 2nd ed. London: British Film Institute, 2005.

Kuritz, Paul. *The Fiery Serpent: A Christian Theory of Film and Theater*. Enumclaw, WA: Pleasant Word, 2007.

Lawhead, Stephen. *Turn Back the Night: A Christian Response to Popular Culture*. Westchester, IL: Crossway Books-Good News Publishers, 1985.

Lewerenz, Spencer and Barbara Nicolosi. *Behind the Screen: Hollywood Insiders on Faith, Film, and Culture*. Grand Rapids, MI: Baker Books, 2005.

Lowry, Eugene. *The Homiletical Plot: The Sermon As Narrative Art Form*. London: Westminster John Knox Press, 2000.

Lubin, David M. *Titanic*. London: British Film Institute, 1999.

Maritain, Jacques. *The Responsibility of the Artist*. Staten Island, NY: Gordian Press, 1972.

Mattingly, Terry. *Pop Goes Religion: Faith in Popular Culture.* Nashville, TN: W Publishing Group, 2005.

McKee, Robert. *Story: Substance, Structure, Style, and the Principles of Screenwriting.* New York: HarperCollins-Regan, 1997.

Medved, Michael. *Hollywood vs. America.* New York: HarperCollins-HarperPerennial, 1992.

Monaco, James. *How to Read a Film: The Art, Technology, Language, History, and Theory of Film and Media.* New York: Oxford University Press, 1981.

Moore, T. M. *Culture Matters: A Call for Consensus on Christian Cultural Engagement.* Grand Rapids, MI: Brazos Press, 2007.

——. *Redeeming Pop Culture: A Kingdom Approach.* Phillipsburg, NJ: P&R Publishing, 2003.

Overstreet, Jeffrey. *Through a Screen Darkly.* Ventura, CA: Regal Books, 2007.

Phillips, Patrick. *Understanding Film Texts: Meaning and Experience.* London: British Film Institute, 2000.

Pollock, Dale. *Skywalking: The Life and Films of George Lucas.* New York: Da Capo Press, 1999.

Reinhartz, Adele. *Jesus of Hollywood.* Oxford: Oxford University Press, 2007.

Romanowski, William D. *Eyes Wide Open: Looking for God in Popular Culture.* Grand Rapids, MI: Brazos Press, 2007.

Rosenstand, Nina. *The Moral of the Story: An Introduction to Ethics.* 5th ed. Boston: McGraw Hill, 2006.

Sanders, Steven, ed. *The Philosophy of Science Fiction Film.* Lexington, KY: The University Press of Kentucky, 2008.

Schaeffer, Franky. *Sham Pearls for Real Swine.* Brentwood, TN: Wolgemuth and Hyatt Publishers, 1990.

Skal, David J. *The Monster Show: A Cultural History of Horror.* New York: Faber and Faber, 1993.

Solomon, Jerry, ed. *Arts, Entertainment, and Christian Values: Probing the Headlines That Impact Your Family.* Grand Rapids, MI: Kregel, 2000.

Stam, Robert. *Film Theory: An Introduction.* Malden, MA: Blackwell, 2000.

Tasker, Yvonne. *The Silence of the Lambs.* London: British Film Institute, 2002.

Vogler, Christopher. *The Writer's Journey: Mythic Structure for Writers.* 2nd ed. Studio City, CA: Michael Wiese Productions, 1998.

Wharton, David and Jeremy Grant. *Teaching Analysis of Film Language.* London: British Film Institute, 2007.

Whedbee, J. William. *The Bible and the Comic Vision.* Minneapolis: Fortress Press, 2002.

Wood, Ralph C. *The Gospel According to Tolkien: Visions of the Kingdom in Middle-earth.* Louisville: Westminster John Knox Press, 2003.

Web Sites

- actoneprogram.com
- christiananswers.net/spotlight
- christianitytoday.com/movies
- churchofthemasses.blogspot.com
- crosswalk.com
- damaris.org
- film-philosophy.com
- hollywoodjesus.com
- imdb.com
- inter-mission.net
- movieministry.com
- mrqe.com
- pluggedinonline.com
- ransomfellowship.org
- relevantmagazine.com
- rottentomatoes.com/movie
- salvomag.com
- simplyscripts.com

PHILOSOPHY, THEOLOGY, ETHICS, EVANGELISM, AND APOLOGETICS

———. *The Archaeology of Palestine.* Baltimore, MD: Penguin, 1949.

Albright, William F. *Archaeology and the Religion of Israel.* Baltimore, MD: The Johns Hopkins Press, 1953.

Aldrich, Joe. *Lifestyle Evangelism.* Sisters, OR: Multnomah Publishers, 1993.

Aquinas, Thomas. *Summa Contra Gentiles.* Translated by Anton Pegis. New York: Image Books, 1955.

Aristotle. *The Basic Works of Aristotle.* Edited by Richard McKeon. New York: Random House, 1941.

Barnett, Paul. *Is the New Testament Reliable?* 2nd ed. Downers Grove, IL: InterVarsity Press, 2003.

Beckwith, Francis J. and Gregory Koukl. *Relativism: Feet Firmly Planted in Mid-Air.* Grand Rapids, MI: Baker Books, 1998.

Black, David Alan. *Why Four Gospels? The Historical Origins of the Gospels.* Grand Rapids, MI: Kregel Academic & Professional, 2001.

Bruce, F. F. *The New Testament Documents: Are They Reliable?* Grand Rapids, MI: Eerdmans, 2003.

Budziszewski, J. *Written on the Heart: The Case for Natural Law.* Downers Grove, IL: InterVarsity Press, 1997.

Comfort, Ray. *Hell's Best Kept Secret.* New Kensington, PA: Whitaker House, 1989.

Copan, Paul. *"That's Just Your Interpretation": Responding to Skeptics Who Challenge Your Faith.* Grand Rapids, MI: Baker Books, 2001.

Craig, William Lane. *The Kalam Cosmological Argument.* Eugene, OR: Wipf and Stock Publishers, 2000.

———. *Reasonable Faith.* Wheaton, IL: Crossway Books, 1994.

Dillow, Joseph C. *Solomon on Sex: The Biblical Guide to Married Love.* Nashville: Thomas Nelson, 1977.

Downs, Tim. *Finding Common Ground: How to Communicate with Those Outside the Christian Community . . . While We Still Can.* Chicago: Moody, 1999.

Foreman, Mark. *Christianity and Bioethics: Confronting Clinical Issues.* Joplin, MS: College Press Publishing Company, 1999.

Geisler, Norman. *Baker Encyclopedia of Christian Apologetics.* Grand Rapids, MI: Baker, 1999.

———. *Christian Ethics: Options and Issues.* Grand Rapids, MI: Baker Books, 1989.

Geisler, Norman and Frank S. Turek III. *I Don't Have Enough Faith to Be an Atheist.* Westchester, IL: Crossway Books-Good News Publishers, 2004.

Geisler, Norman and Thomas Howe. *When Critics Ask.* Wheaton, IL: Victor Books, 1992.

Geisler, Norman and Winfried Corduan. *Philosophy of Religion.* Grand Rapids, MI: Baker Books, 1988.

Geivett, R. Douglas and James S. Spiegel, eds. *Faith, Film, and Philosophy: Big Ideas on the Big Screen.* Downers Grove, IL: IVP Academic, 2007.

Gilson, Etienne. *God and Philosophy.* New Haven, CT: Yale Nota Bene, 2002.

———. *The Unity of Philosophical Experience.* San Francisco: Ignatius, 1964.

Habermas, Gary R. and Michael R. Licona. *The Case for the Resurrection of Jesus.* Grand Rapids, MI: Kregel, 2004.

Holloway, Maurice R. *An Introduction to Natural Theology.* Saint Louis, MO: Saint Louis University, 1959.

Howe, Thomas. *Objectivity in Biblical Interpretation.* Altamonte Springs, FL: Advantage Inspirational, 2005.

Jastrow, Robert. *God and the Astronomers.* New York: W. W. Norton & Company, 2000.

Kennedy, D. James. *Evangelism Explosion.* Carol Stream, IL: Tyndale House, 1996.

Kreeft, Peter. *A Refutation of Moral Relativism.* San Francisco: Ignatius Press, 1999.

——. *The Unaborted Socrates.* Downers Grove, IL: InterVarsity Press, 1983.

Lawrence, Matt. *Like a Splinter in Your Mind: The Philosophy Behind the Matrix Trilogy.* Malden, MA: Blackwell Publishing, 2004.

Lewis, C. S. *Mere Christianity.* New York: Macmillan Publishing Co., 1953.

——. *Miracles.* New York: Touchstone, 1996.

——. *The Problem of Pain.* New York: Touchstone, 1996.

Little, Paul. *How to Give Away Your Faith.* Downers Grove, IL: InterVarsity Press, 1966.

Machuga, Ric. *In Defense of the Soul: What It Means to Be Human.* Grand Rapids, MI: Brazos Press, 2002.

McDowell, Josh. *The New Evidence That Demands a Verdict.* Nashville: Thomas Nelson, 1999.

Metzger, Will. *Tell the Truth: The Whole Gospel to the Whole Person by Whole People.* 3rd ed. Downers Grove, IL: InterVarsity Press, 2002.

Miller, Ed. L. and Jon Jensen. *Questions That Matter: An Invitation to Philosophy.* Boston: McGraw Hill, 2006.

Moreland, J. P. *Love Your God with All Your Mind: The Role of Reason in the Life of the Soul.* Colorado Springs, CO: Navpress, 1997.

——, J. P. *Scaling the Secular City.* Grand Rapids, MI: Baker Book House, 1987.

Porter, Burton F. *Philosophy Through Fiction and Film.* Upper Saddle River, NJ: Pearson, 2004.

Ramsay, Sir William. *St. Paul the Traveller and the Roman Citizen.* New York: G. P. Putnam's Sons, 1896.

Rosenstand, Nina. *The Moral of the Story.* 6th ed. Boston: McGraw Hill, 2009.

Schaeffer, Francis. *The God Who Is There.* Downers Grove, IL: InterVarsity Press, 1998.

Sherwin-White, A. N. *Roman Society and Roman Law in the New Testament.* Oxford: Clarendon, 1963.

Sire, James. *The Universe Next Door: A Basic Worldview Catalog.* Downers Grove, IL: InterVarsity Press, 2004.

Sullivan, Daniel J. *An Introduction to Philosophy: The Perennial Principles of the Classical Realist Tradition.* Rockford, IL: Tan Books, 1992.

WEB SITES

- apologeticsindex.org
- carm.org
- christian-thinktank.com
- dougbeaumont.org
- gotquestions.org
- leaderu.com
- ses.edu
- str.org

NOTES

CHAPTER 1: CAN ANYTHING GOOD COME OUT OF HOLLYWOOD?

1. For the purposes of this discussion we will treat "Hollywood" and "the film industry" as one, although this is certainly an oversimplification.

2. The church has generally followed one or the other. Augustine and Aquinas, for example, were strongly influenced by Plato and Aristotle, respectively.

3. Actually, because the physical world is seen by Plato as a shadow of the higher World of the Forms, art is a representation of a representation!

4. Statistics vary, but seventy hours per week is not unusual. See http://www.allacademic.com; http://americanheart.mediaroom.com; http://news.cnet.com/Teens-and-media-a-full-time-job.

5. From Barbara Nicolosi's weblog, *Church of the Masses*, http://churchofthemasses.blogspot.com.

6. From *The Language of the Night* as cited in Lynette Porter, David Lavery, and Hillary Robson, *Finding Battlestar Galactica: An Unauthorized Guide* (Naperville, IL: Sourcebooks, 2008), 248.

7. The first two are attributed to the Epicureans, followed by Menander, Epimenides, Euripides, and Epimenides/Aratus.

8. The statement "we are his offspring" is either true or false, depending on who "he" refers to. In Paul's case it was the true God and thus the statement was true in Paul's context.

9. Stephen Lawhead, *Turn Back the Night* (Westchester, IL: Crossway Books-Good News Publishing, 1985), 8.

CHAPTER 2: HOW A STORY IS TOLD VS. WHAT A STORY TELLS

10. Robert McKee, *Story: Substance, Structure, Style and the Principles of Screenwriting* (New York: HarperEntertainment, 1997), 114.

11. William D. Romanowski, *Eyes Wide Open: Looking for God in Popular Culture* (Grand Rapids, MI: Brazos Press, 2007), 223.

12. Ibid., 52.

13. Matthew 27:24-25; Acts 2:22-41; 10:34-43

14. Statements Gibson made at other times have suggested some anti-Semitic feelings, however.

15. In these cases the director may choose to use the Director's Guild approved pseudonym "Alan Smithee," an anagram of "the alias men." Actors and actresses may do the same with the alias George or Georgina Spelvin.

16. In some cases filmmakers state that their work means "nothing" at all. One of the creators of *Frailty* (2001) stated in the DVD's extra features that the film's story did not really mean anything—yet its message (one of extreme faith in God) was loud and clear!

CHAPTER 3: STORY: STRUCTURE, SIGHTS, AND SOUNDS

17. Aristotle, *Poetics*, 5.1.

18. Syd Field, *Screenplay: The Foundations of Screenwriting* (New York: Delta, 2005). The classic three-act structure is not the only model available for story structuring. Aristotle himself noted additional plot elements (see *Poetics*, 6.6). For other models, see *Freytag's Technique of the Drama: An Exposition of Dramatic Composition and Art* (1968) by Elias J. MacEwan; www.dsiegel.com; and *The Writer's Journey: Mythic Structures for Writers* (Studio City, CA: Michael Wiese Productions, 2007) by Christopher Vogler. Nevertheless, nearly all stories can be structurally reduced to the classic three-act model as described in this book.

19. McKee, *Story*, 62.

20. See Joseph Campbell, *The Hero with a Thousand Faces* (Princeton, NJ: Princeton University Press, 1973) or (with Bill Moyers) *The Power of Myth* (New York: Anchor Books-Doubleday, 1988). Campbell is often criticized for presenting oversimplified versions of myths and ignoring glaring inconsistencies to support his theory. For example, see Tom Snyder, *Myth Conceptions: Joseph Campbell and the New Age* (Grand Rapids, MI: Baker Books, 1995).

21. From Christopher Vogler, *The Writer's Journey: Mythic Structure for Writers, 2nd ed.* (Studio City, CA: Michael Wiese Productions, 1998), 26.

22. See Donald Rayfield, *Anton Chekhov: A Life* (New York: Henry Holt and Company, 1997).

23. Some make a stronger distinction between "what is in the scene" vs. "how the scene is shot," or *mis-en-scene* vs. *mis-en-shot*. See Warren Buckland, *Film Studies* (London: Hodder and Stoughton, 1998), 10.

CHAPTER 4: STYLE: HOW THE STORY MOVES

24. Kirby Dick reports in his documentary *This Film Is Not Yet Rated* (2006) that the MPAA rates four times as many movies NC-17 for nudity/sexuality than for violence.

25. See MPAA Ratings Explanations at http://www.mpaa.org/FlmRat_Ratings.asp.

26. Michael Medved, *Hollywood vs. America: Popular Culture and the War Against*

Traditional Values (New York: HarperCollins Publishers, 1992), 289.

27. The popular director M. Night Shyamalan, known for being "Mr. PG-13," states in his commentary that the studio asked him to make his 2008 film *The Happening* R-rated.

28. From http://www.mpaa.org/FlmRat_Posters.asp#. Used with permission.

29. Specific texts include Colossians 3:8; Ephesians 4:29; and perhaps principles such as those found in Matthew 15:10-20.

30. Colossians 3:8: "Abusive speech" (NASB) or "filthy language" (NIV). The underlying Greek term ($\alpha\iota\sigma\chi\rho\sigma\lambda\sigma\gamma\iota\alpha$) is used only here in the New Testament and can mean "evil speech in the sense of obscene speech . . . or abusive speech." Paul might have had either, or both, connotations in mind.

31. Joshua 6; 10; Psalm 44; Romans 13; Genesis 14; 1 Samuel 23:1-2.

32. Acts 22:25-29 and 23:23.

33. The argument that it was acceptable to include all the gore because "that's the way it really was" is overstating the case. See Romanowski, *Eyes Wide Open*, 110.

34. For example, in the sniper drama *Shooter* (2007), a man is shot in the head by a .50-caliber rifle from an extreme distance. When the bullet strikes, he falls to the ground and some blood sprays out behind him. Patrick Garrity, who served as the military technical advisor on *Shooter*, had this to say regarding the scene: "Because of the caliber of that round and the hydrostatic shock that follows it, it peels you apart. You have limbs flying two hundred feet away and you're in twenty different pieces. They can't show that in a movie." From "Special Features" interview on *Shooter* DVD.

35. This does not mean that clothing itself is "part of the fall" in the sense that it is evil—for God made Adam and Eve even better clothing soon afterward. Rather, clothing protects us from improperly close relationships. Nudity is not, therefore, a "return to innocence" in a sinful world.

36. Nudity in art was rarely contested by the church until recently. It was not explicitly condemned until the anti-Protestant Council of Trent in the sixteenth century, and even after the Reformation, the Protestant church continued to support artistic uses of nudity, especially when depicting biblical scenes that might demand it for accuracy.

37. A good discussion of this subject can be found in Romanowski, *Eyes Wide Open*, 198-205.

38. We cannot be forced to sin because sin is an act of the will, so temptation alone is not a sin (Hebrews 4:15). But we are responsible for keeping ourselves away from tempting situations that can lead to sin.

39. Acts 15:20; 1 Corinthians 6:18; 10:8; Ephesians 5:3; Colossians 3:5; 1 Thessalonians 4:3.

40. Leviticus 18:22; 20:13; Matthew 19:3-8; Romans 1:26-27; 1 Corinthians 7:6-11.

CHAPTER 5: SUPPOSITIONS: THE WORLD OF THE STORY

41. Robert L. Short, *The Gospel from Outer Space* (London: Fount, 1983), 51.

42. This is similar to the way a Catholic priest is an archetype for "pious religious character." It is not that Hollywood writers know or care to say anything about Roman Catholic dogma; it is simply that they need a recognizable figure to represent a certain kind of character without having to deal with a lot of characterization issues.

43. In the 1980s, a spate of Vietnam War–related movies were released, such as *First Blood* and its *Rambo* sequels (1982, 1985, 1988, 2008); the *Missing in Action* trilogy (1984, 1985, 1988); *Uncommon Valor* (1983); *Platoon* (1986); *Bat 21* (1988); *Full Metal Jacket* (1987); and *Hamburger Hill* (1987). These films ranged from very serious commentary on the conflict to films that almost spoofed their own sub-genre. *First Blood*, for example, was a serious drama focused on the sad plight of a Vietnam veteran who happened into a town that wanted nothing to do with him. The sequels, on the other hand, turned this lonely drifter into an unstoppable killing machine. When the final sequel was released in 2008, Rambo had become a more believable, grounded figure.

44. Robert McKee notes that one of the important features of comedy is the fact that ultimately no one gets hurt (*Story*, 87).

45. The same cannot be said for other media, considering the success of programs like *The Sarah Silverman Show*.

46. In fact, Rowling has also claimed to be a Christian. See http://www.accio-quote.org/articles/2000/1000-vancouversun-wyman.htm.

47. Richard Abanes, *Fantasy and Your Family: Exploring The Lord of the Rings, Harry Potter and Modern Magick* (Camp Hill, PA: Christian Publications, 2002), 194.

48. There were many reports that interest in occultism spiked at the height of these books'/films' popularity. This was certainly not the case with *The Lord of the Rings* or *Narnia*. These results should also raise questions as to the story's influence. Richard Abanes discusses this in *Fantasy and Your Family*.

49. Issues about magic are not often raised regarding *The Golden Compass* (2007), but its inclusion of good witches is of little concern compared to the anti-religious elements that are so clear.

CHAPTER 6: SIGNIFICANCE: THE MORAL OF THE STORY

50. Robert McKee asks in regard to this issue, "Are you convinced of the random meaninglessness of life? If your answer is a passionate yes, then write your Miniplot or Antiplot." He then adds, "For the vast majority, however, the honest answer to these questions is no." McKee, *Story*, 66.

51. For example, Stanley Grenz notes that in order to understand postmodernism, one

need only look at the crews of *Star Trek* and *Star Trek: The Next Generation.* See Stanley J. Grenz, *A Primer on Postmodernism* (Grand Rapids, MI: Eerdmans, 1996), 1-10.

52. In the Campbell/Vogler scheme, the hero and mentor will embody the message of the movie, while threshold guardians and shadows communicate opposing views.

CHAPTER 7: DISCUSSING MOVIES RELIGIOUSLY:
IS SALVATION SELF-REALIZATION OR SINCERE REPENTANCE?

53. In 1994, Michael Medved cited over fifty anti-religion films in an hour-long documentary to demonstrate how Hollywood often treats the subject of religion. See Michael Medved, *Hollywood vs. Religion*, VHS (Dallas: Chatham Hill, 1994).

54. For example Brian Godawa, *Hollywood Worldviews: Watching Films with Wisdom and Discernment* (Downers Grove, IL: Intervarsity Press, 2002), chapter 2; Robert Johnston, *Reel Spirituality: Theology and Film in Dialogue* (Grand Rapids, MI: Baker Academic, 2006), chapters 6 and 8; Vogler, *The Writer's Journey*, 203-236; Romanowski, *Eyes Wide Open*, 156-58; Paul Kuritz, *The Fiery Serpent: A Christian Theory of Film and Theater* (Enumclaw, WA: Pleasant World, 2006), chapter 5.

55. Brian Godawa believes that the nature of story is itself a reflection of the biblical redemption story (a "metanarrative" or "story of stories"). See Godawa, "Movies, Storytelling, and Apologetics," www.nicenecouncil.com/media/display.pl?media_file=11.

56. Ecclesiastes 12:13. Augustine echoed these words centuries later when he wrote in his *Confessions*, "You have made us for yourself, O Lord, and our heart is restless until it rests in you."

57. See John 2:23; 10:25, 38; 14:29.

58. Exodus 4:1-8; 1 Kings 18:36-39; Acts 2:22 and 43; Hebrews 2:3-4; 2 Corinthians 12:12.

CHAPTER 8: DISCUSSING MOVIES PHILOSOPHICALLY:
IS REALITY VIRTUAL OR VERITABLE?

59. For example, if I state that homosexual behavior is sinful, I am stating an objective fact, for sin is acting contrary to God's will and God has stated that homosexual activity is contrary to His will.

60. I am indebted to an enlightening personal conversation with Dr. Matthew Lawrence of Long Beach City College, California, for several portions of this dialogue. For his thoughts on *The Matrix* see his book *Like a Splinter in Your Mind: The Philosophy Behind the Matrix Trilogy* (Malden, MA: Blackwell Publishing, 2004).

61. This issue is too complex to pursue here. However, several books have useful introductory discussions, including Francis J. Beckwith and Gregory Koukl's *Relativism: Feet Firmly Planted in Mid-Air* (Grand Rapids, MI: Baker Books, 1998), and Paul Copan's *That's Just Your Interpretation* (Grand Rapids, MI: Baker Books, 2001).

CHAPTER 9: DISCUSSING MOVIES THEOLOGICALLY:
IS GOD A DELUSION OR DEITY?

62. See William Lane Craig and Quentin Smith, *Theism, Atheism and Big Bang Cosmology* (Oxford: Oxford University Press, 1995); Robert Jastrow, *God and the Astronomers* (New York: Norton, 1978); Stephen Hawking, *A Brief History of Time: From the Big Bang to Black Holes* (New York: Bantam, 1988).

63. For more on this argument see William Lane Craig, *The Kalam Cosmological Argument* (Eugene, OR: Wipf & Stock Publishers, 2000).

64. Robert Jastrow, *God and the Astronomers* (New York: W. W. Norton & Company, 2000), 105-106.

65. Scientists also point out that the vastness of the universe is a prerequisite for life. See Hugh Ross, *The Creator and the Cosmos* (Colorado Springs, CO: NavPress, 2001).

66. For more on the scientific evidence for the beginning of the universe, see Norman L. Geisler and Frank Turek, *I Don't Have Enough Faith to Be an Atheist* (Wheaton, IL: Crossway Books, 2004), especially chapters 3-5.

67. Romans 2:12-15.

68. For more on the moral argument see J. Budziszewski, *Written on the Heart: The Case for Natural Law* (Downers Grove, IL: InterVarsity Press, 1997).

69. C. S. Lewis, *Surprised by Joy* (New York: Harvest/Harcourt, 1966), 120.

70. As quoted in Martin Gardner, *The Whys of a Philosophical Scrivener,* 2nd ed. (New York: St. Martin's Griffin, 1999), 451. Emphasis in original.

71. For more on the argument from desire see Peter Kreeft and Ronald K. Tacelli, *Handbook of Christian Apologetics: Hundreds of Answers to Crucial Questions* (Downers Grove, IL: InterVarsity Press, 1994), 78-81.

CHAPTER 10: DISCUSSING MOVIES SCRIPTURALLY:
IS THE BIBLE MYTHOLOGICAL OR MIRACULOUS?

72. The Warden's framed needlepoint sampler comes into play more than once. It reads, "His Judgment Cometh, and That Right Soon." The verse may come from the apocryphal book of Sirach 21:5, which ends with, "and his judgment comes speedily" (NRSV).

73. Concerning the numerous falsehoods in the book and film, see Richard Abanes, *The Truth Behind the Da Vinci Code: A Challenging Response to the Bestselling Novel* (Eugene, OR: Harvest House Publishers, 2004).

74. "There were specifications not only for the kind of skins to be used and the size of the columns, but there was even a religious ritual necessary for the scribe to perform before writing the name of God. Rules governed the kind of ink used, dictated the spacing of words, and prohibited writing anything from memory. The lines, and even the letters, were counted methodically. If a manuscript was found to contain even one mistake, it was discarded and destroyed. This scribal formalism was responsible, at least in part, for the extreme care exercised in copying the Scriptures. It was also the reason there were only a few manuscripts (as the rules demanded the destruction of defective copies)." Norman Geisler, *The Baker Encyclopedia of Christian Apologetics* (Grand Rapids, MI: Baker Academic, 1998), 550-54.

75. For more on the copy reliability of the Bible, see Paul Barnett, *Is the New Testament Reliable?* (Downers Grove, IL: InterVarsity Press, 2005), and F. F. Bruce, *The New Testament Documents: Are They Reliable?* (Grand Rapids, MI: Eerdmans, 2003).

76. Geisler, *Baker Encyclopedia of Christian Apologetics*, 381-85.

77. For good introductions to the topic of biblical archeology see *The Archeological Study Bible* (Grand Rapids, MI: Zondervan, 2005); Josh McDowell, *Evidence That Demands a Verdict*, 369-88; Geisler, *Baker Encyclopedia of Christian Apologetics*, 46-52; and Geisler and Brooks, *When Skeptics Ask: A Handbook on Christian Evidences* (Grand Rapids, MI: Baker Books, 2008), 179-208.

78. See Sir William Ramsay, *St. Paul the Traveller and the Roman Citizen* (New York: G. P. Putnam's Sons, 1896), 8.

79. See "William Albright: Toward a More Conservative View," in *Christianity Today*, 18 January 1963.

80. A. N. Sherwin-White, *Roman Society and Roman Law in the New Testament: The Sarum Lectures 1960-1961* (Eugene, OR: Wipf & Stock Publishers, 2004), 189.

81. See also Dan Graves, *Scientists of Faith: 48 Biographies of Historic Scientists and Their Christian Faith* (Grand Rapids, MI: Kregel, 1996). Also Eric C. Barrett and David Fisher, *Scientists Who Believe: 21 Tell Their Own Stories* (Chicago: Moody Press, 1984).

82. A brief list of the problems with evolutionary theory includes false ape-men, the problem of biogenesis, the design inference, accounting for the Cambrian Explosion, the paucity of the fossil record, problems in genetics, an explanation for irreducible complexity, as well as several philosophical issues. Scientists can be found in every field that have issues with the theory. For examples see http://www.dissentfromdarwin.org; http://www.intelligentdesignnetwork.org/; http://discoverycsc.org/; http://www.iconsofevolution.com/. For some philosophical problems see Alvin Plantinga, *Warranted Christian Belief* (Oxford: Oxford University Press, 2000), chapter

7; Etienne Gilson, *From Aristotle to Darwin and Back Again* (Lanham, MD: Sheed and Ward, 1984); Ric Machuga, *In Defense of the Soul: What It Means to Be Human* (Grand Rapids, MI: Brazos Press, 2002).

83. See http://www.leaderu.com/cyber/books/pensees/pensees.html.

84. See John Warry, *Alexander: 334-323 B.C.* (Westport, CT: Praeger, 2005).

85. Psalm 22:16 (cf. Luke 23:33); Zechariah 12:10 (cf. John 19:34); Psalm 22:18 (cf. John 19:23-24).

86. Luke 21 (cf. Matthew 24 and Mark 13).

87. See Gary R. Habermas and Michael R. Licona, *The Case for the Resurrection of Jesus* (Grand Rapids, MI: Kregel, 2004).

88. 1 Corinthians 15:58.

CHAPTER 11: WHAT SHOULD WE THEN WATCH?

89. See the NKJV, NASB, NIV, and NET translations for examples of the better rendering.

90. Matthew 15; Mark 2; Luke 5:27-32; 7:36-50; 15:1-10; 19:1-10; John 12:1-7.

91. 1 Peter 2:22; 1 John 3:5.

92. Romans 14 and 1 Corinthians 8-10.

93. Romans 14:13-23; cf. 1 Corinthians 8.

94. Philippians 1:9-11; 1 Thessalonians 3:10.